Randolph Charles

D0725393

The Anglican Tradition

THE ANGLICAN TRADITION

Richard Holloway, editor

Morehouse-Barlow Co., Inc. Wilton, Connecticut
Anglican Book Centre   Toronto, Canada

Copyright © 1984 Richard Holloway

All rights reserved. No part of this publication may be
reproduced, stored in a retrieval system, or transmitted in any
form or by any means, electronic, mechanical, photocopying,
recording, or otherwise, without the prior permission of the
copyright owner.

Morehouse-Barlow Co., Inc.
78 Danbury Road
Wilton, Connecticut 06897

and in Canada:
Anglican Book Centre
600 Jarvis Street
Toronto, Ontario M4Y-2J6

Morehouse-Barlow Co. ISBN 0-8192-1338-1
Anglican Book Centre ISBN 0-919891-10-1

Library of Congress Catalog Card Number 83-62541

Printed in the United States of America

Contents

Chapter 1
Anglicanism:
A Church Adrift?

1

Anglicanism: A Church Adrift?

by Richard Holloway

I HAD a letter from a friend recently. Half in jest, half seriously, I suspect, he quoted someone as having said: "The great thing about being a member of the Anglican Church is that it does not interfere with your politics or your religion." We can take that paradoxical statement in two ways. We can take it dismissively: Anglicanism means nothing and makes no demands. It's really only a kind of ethnic or cultural style. On the surface it has a kind of gloss (although that has been severely scratched in recent years), but underneath there is nothing of substance, nothing solid and enduring. Anglicanism is essentially a rather charming veneer, carefully lacquered on cardboard. It looks impressive from a slight distance, but once you really test it, put some pressure on it, it collapses.

Or you can take this statement approvingly: the Anglican Church is a tolerant, faintly detached and amused mother of lazily permissive standards, but she is a real mother, nevertheless. She does not hector and bully her children. She expects them to be mature and independent. There are certain house rules she likes observed in her home, a sort of minimal but important standard, but if her children break it she doesn't go into an operatic tantrum. She merely raises her eyebrows and wishes they had better manners. Anglicans are not persecutors or excommunicators. We tend to agree with Montaigne, that it is rating our conjectures highly to roast people alive for them.

Now, each of these perspectives on Anglicanism has something to be said for it. Anglicanism is not, at first sight, a very demanding religion. It lacks the absolutist impulse, that passion for the highest that characterizes many religions. We lack that. We are not a very heroic church. We don't produce many blazing examples of the kind of sanctity that consumes the subject in a lifetime of self-surrender, such as the great Roman Catholic saints of the Counter-Reformation or, nearer our own day, the great Curé d'Ars in nineteenth-century France, who lived on cold potatoes and had to spend most of his time in the confessional because sinners came to him from all over Europe, so sanctifying was his influence. In our own day the most shining example is probably Mother Teresa of Calcutta, who is so holy that her influence is even felt at Harvard. We lack that heroic, absolutist impulse. Anglican clergy certainly lack it. We have been described as "the bland leading the bland". On the whole, we are fairly worldly in the Anglican priesthood. Sometimes we are moderately corrupt. Sometimes we are poised uneasily between this world and the Unseen world. More often, we are quite comfortably ensconced in this world. Rarely are we so completely caught up into the Unseen world that, in Paul's phrase, this world becomes as refuse.

On the other hand, at our best there is something to be said for us. There is a moderation and reasonableness about Anglicanism, a sort of modest kindliness that has something of the gentleness of God in it. If we have an Old Testament standard, it is surely Psalm 103.

"The Lord is full of compassion and mercy, long-suffering and of great goodness. He will not always be chiding; neither keepeth he his anger for ever. He hath not dealt with us after our sins; nor rewarded us according to our wickednesses. For look how high the heaven is in comparison of the earth; so great is his mercy also towards them that fear him. Look how wide also the east is from the west; so far hath he set our sins from us. Yea, like as a father pitieth his own children; even so is the Lord merciful unto them that fear him. For he knoweth whereof we are made; he remembereth that we are but dust".

And as Father Stanton used to say, "you can't always expect dust to be up to the mark". There *is* a genuine type of Anglican sanctity: modest and homely, in the English sense of that word. George Herbert and John Keble are supreme examples of that kind of holiness. Each had a kind of limpid spirituality that was almost childlike in its straightforwardness.

So we are not a church for everyone, which is why really ardent extremists of one sort or another find us exasperating. People who like a well-chiseled definition in doctrine and ethics will find us irritating, because we have a debilitating weakness for seeing the other side of the question. And this very moderateness and reasonableness places us in a great danger. Some other churches may be in danger of using the Gospel as an instrument of terror or coercion (every Anglican priest is often called upon to counsel people from more absolutist churches whose lives and souls have been damaged by the blunt and uncompromising way they've been taught). The danger of the absolutists in religion—whom Ronald Knox called 'ultrasupernaturalists'—is that they have too tight a grip on the Gospel, and they often use it like a blunt instrument to hit people with. Our danger is different. Our grip on the Gospel is sometimes so slack and listless that we are often in danger of letting it slip away from us altogether. This is why we must constantly listen to the warnings of scripture.

The Letter to the Hebrews always sounds a timely warning for Anglicans. It tells us: "We must pay the closer attention to what we have heard least we drift away from it" (2.1). This metaphor of drifting or slipping can be taken in two ways. In the text it can refer to a boat that is gently floating past a safe landing place and is in danger of drifting downstream away from its own secure haven. Or it can refer to a rather loosely fitting ring, which can easily slip off our finger and be lost because of our inattentiveness.

We don't know who the author of Hebrews was or to whom or when he sent his letter. In fact, we are not sure if it is a letter, at all. It has all the pace and rhetorical power of a great sermon. Maybe it was delivered as a sermon and then sent on to another group. The Church described it as a letter to 'the Hebrews' because of its content. Its hearers or recipients seem to be Jewish Christians. At any rate, it is assumed that they know a lot about the Old Testament and its liturgical and sacrificial traditions. The main point of the letter is straightforward. The writer is afraid that his readers will fall into the sin of apostasy, of repudiating the Faith and denying Jesus Christ, the object of faith. The readers were probably Jews of the diaspora living somewhere outside the Holy Land; perhaps, even, in Rome. They had never known Jesus. It is likely that they had never known anyone who had seen him, any of the origi-

nal apostolic witnesses. Maybe they were second
or third generation members of a Jewish Christian synagogue. They had inherited, along with
their Jewish traditions, a faith in Jesus as the
long-expected Messiah or Christ. So far, their faith
hadn't cost them much. It was something they had
effortlessly inherited, and it had never been really
tested. It was a rather soft and indefinite thing,
almost childish in its immaturity. And the writer
is anxious for them. He sees a time of real trial
coming, a wave of persecution. So far, they have
not had to face bloodshed. Soon they will. And he's
afraid they'll fall away. They'll simply lapse back
into their old Jewish traditions, because Jesus
means so little to them. Their grip is slack, so the
faith will slip from them like a ring off a finger.
They'll drift into a profound and dangerous apostasy, like a boat that slips its moorings and
drifts out to sea. And what peril they'll be placed
in then! He reminds them of the institution of the
Old Testament law and the religion of Moses, and
the awful penalties God exacted against those
who broke that covenant. The covenant in Christ
is as much greater than the old covenant as God is
greater than Moses. If apostasy from that partial
and temporary covenant was dangerous, how
much more dangerous will be apostasy from the
final and full disclosure of God in Christ. "How
shall we escape if we neglect so great a salvation?" (2.3). So he writes to build them up, to
prepare them for the great testing that is to come
upon them soon.

Now, Anglicanism strikes me as being a bit like
the religion of those Christian Hebrews: deco-
rously ceremonial, often a bit childish in its de-
pendence upon secondary matters, and very slack
in its grip upon the really essential core of the
Christian Faith, what C. S. Lewis called 'mere

Christianity', that irreducible minimum of theology and behavior without which you are not really a Christian at all. So, Anglicans, too, are in great danger. Our danger is unlikely to be of the sort that faced the Hebrews: an actual and systematic persecution by civil authority. Our trial, our testing is much more subtle. The mind of the world gradually erodes our grip on basic Christian Faith and we drift into a kind of Christianity that is purely formal and external. All our standards are derived, not from Christ, but from the world and from society. Without knowing it, we have committed apostasy. We have drifted out to sea.

The word 'apostasy' used to have a chilling and final ring to it. It suggested some grand act of renunciation or craven act of treason, something dark and dramatic, like the work of Judas, who goes and hangs himself in terrible remorse. Alas, it is rarely like this. Really dangerous apostasy is almost effortless and unconscious. It is drift. The word apostasy means to stand against or in opposition to, but that can happen so gradually that you hardly realize it. You cease to stand with Christ, but you don't recognize it. You stand against him and with the world, but you haven't realized it or acknowledged it, or paid much attention to it. When John Keble accused England of national apostasy in 1833, he did not mean it had committed some clearly intended act of repudiation of the Christian Faith. No, England had drifted so far away from a true understanding of the nature of the Faith and the character of the Church that it no longer stood with Christ. Now, it stood for something else. The sense of the Church as the presence in the world of the supernatural Christ had gradually evaporated and been replaced by something else. And there was a lot to be said for that 'something else'. It had a kind of historical continuity with the towering presence of the supernatural Christ: it was a trace or an echo or an aftertaste of that grand reality, but it wasn't the reality itself. It was not Jesus, it was something else, something human, often something fine, something that stood to help preserve the structure of the nation, something to which men's affectionate remembrances clung—but it was not Jesus, nor the Church that mysteriously represented his presence in time. They had drifted away from that, as we can drift from it. We can retain the form, the vocabulary, the charming externals of the Faith, while voiding the whole thing of significant content. During the 1960s some theologians did this intentionally. They tried to provide their generation with what was called the *secular* meaning of the gospel, because no other meaning was possible. Man had become radically secular, had come of age in a world from which God had been banished. Daddy was no longer needed, since we'd all grown up. The official word had been proclaimed by the high priests of the new secular culture, then certain theologians went to work. They retranslated the Christian vocabulary into secular terms, but they kept the ancient words around, the way some people hang old coaching lamps on their suburban villas—as carefully electrified reminders of a primitive past. But they were only kept for decorative purposes. They no longer meant anything. That was definite, intentional apostasy, though it called itself 'secular Christianity'. Today, it is a bit more subtle. It is drift rather than outright denial.

The Oxford fathers, in a day not terribly unlike our own, sought to establish one thing above all others: the divine nature of the Church. That is a truth we must lay hold of again. The Church exists, primarily, not to make us good or to improve

the world or to uphold the state or even to over-
throw it, but to witness to the adorable, objective
reality of God and to give him praise. We exist to
bear witness to a fact, the most overwhelming of
all facts: the glorious reality of God, beside which
all our programs for anything else at all become,
in Paul's words, so much refuse. This was the
great truth to which the Oxford Apostles pointed.
Theirs was a profoundly conservative revolution.
They drew men away from themselves and toward God. They reaffirmed the supernatural
character of the Church. They had their own politics and prejudices and they were wrong about a
number of worldly things, but those things are
forgotten. What endures and still captivates us
and fills us with longing is their power of adoration, their reverence, their silence, their fearful-
ness, their sense of awe before the great and
overwhelming fact of God and the Church as the
covenanted place of his abiding. In words from
Hebrews, "They endured as seeing him who is in-
visible". That is what comes through their sermons and their holy lives. It comes through others
too, and I want to quote quite fully from another
of these witnesses to the reality of God above all
else, Baron von Hügel. Here are three quotations
that capture this fundamental truth:

"... There is so little realisation, so little
stress upon, the primary end and function,
surely, of every Church deserving of the
august name—the awakening of souls to, the
preparing them for, the holding before them
embodiments of, *the other life*, the life beyond the grave. Very certainly the Church
has also to help in the amelioration of *this
life*; but, I submit, always after, and in subor-
dination to, and penetrated by, that metaphysical, ontologial, otherworldly sense and

life which alone completes and satisfies fully awakened man. And only thus shall we be in a position to be fair to the Church's work in the past; for the first object and range of this her care and labours will, and ought to be, distinct from and beyond social improvements".[1]

"You appeal to righteousness, to the hunger for moral perfection, as the easy, true way to religion, and Catholicism—and this as though there were always an identity between morality and religion. I should answer; "For propaedeutic purposes, yes; intrinsically, no". I feel confident that the two are not, *at bottom*, the same thing, nor even different stages of the same thing. Religion, I feel more and more, is (in contrast with Ethics) essentially concerned with what *already* is and most speedily will be, and with what is indeed environing and penetrating man ever on and on, but yet as super-human, other than simply human, as truly transcendent, and not only immanent".[2]

"When Thekla says 'religion has primarily to do with isness not oughtness', she means that religion is essentially evidential; that it intimates, first of all, that a superhuman world, a superhuman reality *is*, exists. The first and central act of religion is *adoration*, sense of God. His otherness though nearness, His distinctness from all finite beings, though not separateness—aloofness—from them".[3]

Is that the primary witness of the Church today? Do men and women get from us even a whiff of the great reality of God? Is there any sense in which we are perceived as men and women who have seen God and been blinded by the sight so that our faces shine and the rest of the world is now seen in a strange and wistful twilight? Is the

Church really priest to the world, does it speak of God, bear even a reflection of that unseen but adorable glory? Is the Church any longer priest to the world or has it become scold, judge, social worker, echo, fellow-traveler, slavish imitator, anything, anything at all, but what it is sent to be: the place where the world catches the rumor of God, the place where the great and eternal longing of humanity for God is, in some wise, satisfied. That is what they got from the Oxford fathers, that sense that beyond them lay the land of their own desire, the lost land of the Trinity, so a whole generation was able to say to them: "Show us the Father and it will satisfy us". Can they say that to us today, or have we ourselves drifted a long way past that simple affirmation?

I think we have, most of us, drifted past it. I think there are two things that erode and eat away at the Church's primary task, and I *suggest* them rather than offer a systematic analysis of them. The first agent of erosion is the critical assault of the clever upon the simple affirmations of faith. The Christian Church has never lacked intellectual champions who were able to defend the faith and find new ways of converting the minds of each generation. There is always tension here, of course, partly because believers are often frightened and not very clever, and partly because the clever are often oversure of themselves and of very little else. Elizabeth Wordsworth summed up the situation perfectly:

> If only the good were the clever,
>   If only the clever were good,
> The world would be better than ever
>   We thought that it possibly could.
> But, alas, it is seldom or never
>   That either behave as they should;

For the good are so harsh to the clever,
The clever so rude to the good.

Even after we have made every allowance possible, it remains a fact that there has been a fairly systematic and devastating effective critical assault upon Christian doctrine during the last several generations. Not the least depressing thing about it has been that most of the demolition work has been conducted by those of our own household. And I'm not talking about the outworks of the citadel of faith, or its ornamentation or embellishments. I'm talking about the foundation elements, the essentials of Faith, what C. S. Lewis called 'mere Christianity'. The real scandal has not been that the assault has come, but that it has come, more or less, from within. Something Walter Pater said in 1888 still applies here:

> "The priest is still, and will, we think, remain one of the necessary types of humanity; and he is untrue to his type, unless, with whatever inevitable doubts in this doubting age, he feels, on the whole, the preponderance in it of those influences which make for faith . . . We have little patience with those liberal clergy who dwell on nothing else than the difficulties of faith and the propriety of concession to the opposite force".[4]

You can agree with that without having a very high opinion of Pater. What we need is an affirming Church that celebrates the reality of God. Difficulties there always will be, but as Cardinal Newman pointed out, "ten thousand difficulties do not make one doubt". During another period of doubt and confusion, Bishop Charles Gore set himself to write 'a reconstitution of Christian Be-

lief'. He wrote three volumes and a fourth in reply
to published criticisms. We need something like
that again, though not necessarily in that form.
We need to repossess the great centralities of our
faith and interpret them anew to our generation
as our fathers did in the past.

If the critical assault upon Christian doctrine is
eroding the very building blocks of the faith, the
moralistic assault of the neo-puritans of Left and
Right is eroding our unity and sapping our energy.
By the moralistic assault, I mean that attempt to
turn the *Isness* of Christian Faith into the *Oughtness* of carefully selective versions of social and
political action. The great indicatives of Christian
Truth imply certain correlative imperatives,
though they are always derivatives and rarely
have the clarity and simplicity of the great revealed truths. I know, because the tradition tells
me, that I am to love God and my neighbor as
myself. I can celebrate the great indicative with
adoration, bowing before the great I AM. Following the great I OUGHT is, for reasons known only to
the Divine Mercy, far more complicated. It is for
that reason that Christian moral axioms are so
few and so general. But we are now in a situation
where we are told exactly what a Christian ought
to do and think and act upon, on a whole spec-
trum of issues from the economic organization of
the state to complex matters of social and sexual
legislation. These moralistic pressures come from
Right and Left. They all have this in common: they
assert that plenary theological authority belongs
only to their point of view, which is usually selective and highly partisan. Moral enthusiasts
always do this. They insist that they have,
somehow, encompassed the wholeness of the
Christian ethic within their own current enthu-
siasms. Bishop Hensley Henson observed:

"Has the pace of moral progress been accel-
erated by Christianity? But this question as-
sumes that there has been moral progress, an
assumption which is obviously disputable,
and which has in fact been vigorously dis-
puted. Is not what we call moral progress
more truly described as a shifting of emphasis on the constituents of morality? In one
age the stress is laid on *purity*; in another on
truth; in another on *liberty*; in another on
charity. But the balance of virtue is never
preserved. The ascetics are hard as nails; the
saints are inquisitors; the theologians care
nothing for freedom; and the humanitarians
are free-thinking and licentious!"[5]

Here I would like to offer a figure to illustrate
the point I am trying to make. Think of the Christian Revelation and its impact and implications as
a dart board or archery target. The 'bull's eye' at
the center is the authoritative core of revealed
truth. Only this are we allowed to proclaim
without compromise and modification, 'In the
name of the Father and of the Son and of the Holy
Ghost'. That core is surprisingly small, and for
many modern Christians it seems hard to find.
Round it in a widening series of circles, becoming
easier to see and hit upon, are the implications,
connections and consequences of this central,
authoritative core. The fascinating thing is that
each section in any of these widening circles is
equidistant from the center, both on the left side
of the board and on the right. They are all certainly related to the center, but none can claim to
be the only consequence or implication of the
revelation. God alone sees the whole dart board.
Most of us are off to one side, some far out, some
closer to center. Our point of view is partial and
perspectival. I believe that this means we should

bring to moral and political debate a strong sense of the ambiguities and provisional nature of what we are doing. We are rarely able to claim concrete specificity for a Christian moral judgment.

One of the paradoxes of the present situation is that many Christian leaders speak with magisterial certainty on social and political and ethical matters of considerable complexity and ambiguity, while they speak with hesitancy and equivocation about matters that relate to the central elements of revealed truth. I'm quite sure that one of the tasks that we ought to turn our hands to is the rediscovery and reconstruction of the order and ordering of Christian truth. We must rediscover and reaffirm what is primary and central, and then proclaim it with joyous conviction. Then we must identify what is secondary or tertiary or derivative, and learn to live with the differences of emphasis and approach that this recognition will inevitably bring. The Anglican Church used to pride itself on cleaving to the great central truths, while allowing freedom of approach and emphasis on secondary matters. We must try to rediscover both the conviction that characterized the former; and the tolerance that characterized the latter.

This little book is a modest attempt to celebrate the central affirmations of the Anglican Tradition. It was delivered as a series of lectures at the Church of the Advent in Boston in 1983, when we celebrated the centenary of our present building and the sesquicentennial of the Oxford Movement. The Oxford Apostles were by no means infallible in their judgment upon events, but their courage and sanctity created a movement of the Spirit that cleansed and invigorated the Anglican Church throughout the world. As part of our celebrations, therefore, we decided to spend some time thinking about the theological, liturgical and spiritual riches of Anglicanism. We called the series of lectures "The Anglican Tradition". We were honored to have such a distinguished group of scholars to guide us through it. And we are glad to share them with a wider audience.

Chapter 2
The Anglican
Theological Tradition

2

The Anglican Theological Tradition

by John Macquarrie

IS THERE such a thing as an Anglican theological tradition? I believe that there is, but it is hard to define, and so there is some excuse for those critics who say that Anglicanism has no distinctive theology and that on doctrinal matters "anything goes" within the Anglican communion.

It is, of course, true that there are no detailed statements of Anglican doctrinal positions comparable either to the dogmas and other authoritative pronouncements received by the Roman Catholic Church and conveniently collected in Denzinger's *Enchiridion Symbolorum* or to the many "confessions of faith" put out by the various Protestant bodies at the time of the Reformation and the subsequent period and each stating a distinctive denominational position. Anglicans have not felt it incumbent on them to spell out doctrine quite so explicitly. This may be partly due to the fact that they have never thought of themselves as separating from the catholic Church, and so it has been maintained that Anglican doctrine is simply the doctrine of the whole Church, not that of some particular tradition. To some, this might seem an arrogant claim, but it appears to receive some recognition in the decree on ecumenism of Vatican II, where it is stated that among the communions stemming from the Reformation, "the Anglican communion occupies a special place," because of its retention of catholic traditions and institutions.[1] However, it may be that the absence in Anglicanism of detailed doctrinal statements is due quite as much to the somewhat empirical and pragmatic temper of the English people. In modern times, at any rate, there has been a distrust of over-precision in doctrinal matters and a recognition that theological statements are bound to have a more or less provisional character. The hesitation in the face of attempts at doctrinal formulation is evidenced not only in the official attitude of Anglicanism but also by the fact that few individual Anglican theologians have engaged in systematic theology. They have tended to be suspicious of "systems," thinking perhaps that they are intellectually too ambitious or that they prematurely "freeze" Christian truth in propositional form, so preventing further exploration. That this fear is quite unfounded may easily be seen by reading the works of continental dogmaticians, both Catholic and Protestant. Schleiermacher and Rahner are good illustrations of men who have not shirked the problems of systematic theology but have clearly recognized the provisional character of their undertaking.

But while the majority of Anglicans have been happy to refrain from close dogmatic definition, it does not follow that there is no recognizable Anglican position in theology or even a distinctively Anglican way of going about the theological task. For instance, just by belonging to the World Council of Churches, the Church of England declares itself to be a church that believes in the Triune God. It may in fact contain theologians who do not so believe, but this is a testimony to the remarkable freedom and tolerance in matters theological enjoyed within the Church of England, and cannot be interpreted as meaning that unitarianism has the same status as trinitarianism in this Church. The individual theologian has distanced himself in certain matters from the teaching of his Church. The Church—for good reasons—does not disown him, but neither does it endorse his teaching, for in its own daily liturgy it continues to proclaim its trinitarian faith.

From time to time, however, Anglicans are forced to be more forthcoming about where they stand in matters of theological belief. One of the most fruitful occasions on which this happened was in the inter-war years—I mean the setting up by the Archbishops of Canterbury and York in 1922 of a Commission on Christian Doctrine, whose report, *Doctrine in the Church of England,* was published in 1938. The occasion for the setting up of this commission was the general feeling that World War I had ended an era and that the Church must address itself to the question of how to express its beliefs in the strange new world of the twentieth century. There were more specific spurs to reflection. The Lambeth Conference of 1920 had opened up serious ecumenical discussions, and it was necessary for the Church of England to define its position in relation to other bodies with whom it might find itself in conversation. Again, there was considerable party strife in the Church, with rather extreme sacramentalist views being put forward by the Anglo-Catholic Congress on the one hand and a minimizing christology by the Modern Churchmen's Union on the other. A good deal of pressure had to be put on the Archbishop of Canterbury (at that time, Randall Davidson) before he agreed to the appointment of the commission. He was prey to the common Anglican anxiety that definition of docrine is unnecessary and likely to be divisive, and Davidson's concern was chiefly to keep the boat from rocking.

However, the commission was in fact appointed, and it is interesting to note its terms of reference: "To consider the nature and grounds of Christian doctrine with a view to demonstrating the extent of existing agreement within the Church of England and with a view to investigating how far it is possible to remove or diminish existing differences."[2] These words imply that the business of the commission was to present a factual report on what is actually believed in the Church rather than a normative statement of the Church's official belief. But in the actual report, there is inevitably some blurring of the distinction between these two different types of statement. The aim was to appoint to the commission younger theologians representing the main traditions in the Church, and to allow them ten to twenty years for carrying out their task. Of the twenty-five members, all were male, twenty-one were clergy and all except one were products of Oxford or Cambridge. The chairman was Bishop Burge, of Oxford, but he died in the early stages and was succeeded by the Bishop of Manchester, at that time William Temple.

Though its authors made only modest claims for it and though it aroused criticism among many who felt that it went too far in acknowledging the legitimacy of a measure of pluralism in matters of doctrine within Anglicanism, the most competent judges have agreed that the report of 1938 is of its kind masterly. More than fifty years after its appearance, one still finds it quoted by Anglican participants in ecumenical dialogues as representing the position of their communion. It was reprinted in 1982 with an extensive introduction by Geoffrey Lampe, which he concluded by quoting as "words that remain true" the comment made by a former Bishop of Manchester in 1938:

"It will be for a very long while a book which will help those who study it to reassert the faith and to exercise considerateness in so doing, and at the same time to preserve that freedom of thought and inquiry which has always been part of the Anglican tradition."[3] It is, of course, true that a document composed in the early part of our century cannot answer all the questions being asked at its close. Yet it is also true that in theology the same questions keep coming back, even if in altered form. Thus Geoffrey Lampe points out that most of the arguments over christology aroused by the book called *The Myth of God Incarnate* (1978) had been anticipated in the controversy initiated by the Modern Churchmen's Union in the events that led up to the appointment of the Archbishops' Commission on Doctrine in 1922, while the ecumenical discussions over church, ministry and sacraments still center on issues that are admirably treated, from an Anglican point of view, in the document of 1938.

In the report itself, after a brief introduction, something is said about the sources of Christian doctrine. Pride of place is given to scripture, and this is surely true to the Anglican tradition. But the doctrine of the verbal inerrancy of scripture is explicitly denied, and the writers make it clear that for them recognition of the authority of scripture is by no means incompatible with a critical approach. Next, the Church is mentioned as a source of doctrine, and again it is true to the Anglican tradition to allow a place to tradition alongside that of scripture. We read: "All Christians are bound to allow very high authority to doctrines which the Church has been generally united in teaching; for each believer has a limited range, and the basis of the Church's belief is far wider than that of his own can ever be. An individual Christian who rejects any part of that belief is guilty of presumption, unless he feels himself bound in conscience to do so and has substantial reasons for holding that what he rejects is not essential to the truth and value of Christianity."[4] The main body of the report falls into three parts: the first is on the doctrines of God and redemption; the second on the church and sacraments; the third on eschatology. One can hardly fail to be struck by the disproportion in length of these three parts. The section on church, ministry and sacraments gets more space than the other two put together—102 pages, as against 58 for God and redemption and a mere 18 for eschatology! We shall later see something of the reason for this Anglican preoccupation with ecclesiology, but we can see that it gives some support to the gibe that one can be a good Anglican if one believes in episcopacy, no matter how much else one disbelieves!

In 1978 there appeared a timely book by Stephen Sykes, entitled *The Integrity of Anglicanism*. Sykes made the straightforward claim that, in spite of all the waffling, "the present Anglican church has incorporated a regular doctrinal structure in the content of its liturgy and in the rules governing its public performance."[5] This point, by the way, was rather similar to one expressed by an Advisory Committee of the American Church, on which I had served myself. This committee had been appointed at the beginning of 1967 by the then Presiding Bishop (John E. Hines) to advise on the theological situation that had arisen out of some of the rather far out utterances of Bishop James Pike, and the threat by some of his fellow bishops to prosecute him for heresy. Perhaps, as in England more than forty years earlier, the main concern of the church leaders was to defuse the situation and avoid the adverse publicity that would have been caused by any heresy trial. Nevertheless, the deliberations of the committee were very useful, and led to the publication of the report entitled *Theological Freedom and Social Responsibility.* This document gave encouragement to theological speculation and disclaimed any wish to "uphold a narrow verbal orthodoxy which requires a person to give literal assent to some particular formulation of doctrine," but went on to say: "We do believe that if an individual finds himself unable, in good conscience, to identify with the living tradition of the church, reflected in the Bible, the creeds, and, especially for Anglicans, in the liturgy of the Book of Common Prayer, he should as a matter of personal integrity voluntarily remove himself from any position in which he might be taken to be an official spokesman for the whole community."[6] So in both the passages quoted, the liturgy and the way of doing it is seen as decisive. There may be no documents that spell out precisely the content of Anglican belief in the form of a confession of faith, but what people do is sometimes better evidence of their inward beliefs than what they say. Actually, Anglicanism has been rather strict in matters of practice, even when it seems lax in expounding the theology behind these practices. For instance, it has insisted throughout its history on an invariable practice of episcopal ordination, and this does imply a conception of ministry, though there could be some variation when it came to formulating this in words. Again, the practice of reverently consuming the consecrated gifts at the end of the eucharist does imply some eucharistic theology, and although this too could be formulated in quite a number of ways, it is obviously a very different theology from that which prevails in those Protestant churches where any bread and wine left over is thrown in the trashcan or poured down the sink. Whether, however, practice alone is adequate to define doctrine is a question that we must raise later.

I said that Stephen Sykes' book was a timely one for it came out just on the eve of the Lambeth Conference of 1978. That conference (like so many others) was meeting in a time of theological confusion. There was renewed controversy over christological issues. A number of ecumenical discussions in different parts of the Anglican communion had come to nothing. Matters had not been much helped by the publication in 1976 of *Christian Believing*, the report of a Doctrine Commission that had been set up by the Archbishops of Canterbury and York ten years earlier. I was myself a member of that commission from 1970 onward, and I think I am correct in saying that I remember it as a group of individualists. Its members were accustomed to make set speeches that were often quite lengthy and rarely related to one another. There was very little in the way of genuine discussion. As was noted both in the foreword by Donald Coggan and in the preface by Maurice Wiles (who had succeeded Ian Ramsey as chairman of the commission), the brief unanimous statement that forms the principal part of the report had been arrived at only with the greatest difficulty and is mainly concerned to stress the fluidity and pluralism that characterize contemporary theology. One of the members of the commission, Geoffrey Lampe, describes its report as a "plea for coexistence," and says that "it suggests that unity in the future will be a unity in asking questions rather than agreeing to answers."[7] This is not a very happy prospect, if the Church thinks it has anything to say to contemporary society. There was in fact general disappointment with the report. Lampe reminds us that it was never discussed in the councils of the Church, never commended to the Church at large, attracted little public comment and, as he put it, was quietly and rapidly buried.[8]

Archbishop Coggan lost no time in appointing a new commission, with an almost entirely different membership, presumably in the hope of getting more positive results. The chairman this time was John Taylor, Bishop of Winchester, and *Believing in the Church* was the deliberately ambiguous title of the report that the new commission issued in 1981. A major concern of the commission was the corporate nature of faith, and how the corporate faith of the Church is related to the varieties of faith found among individual members. There seems to have been some danger that questions about the truth and falsehood of doctrine might be submerged in the idea that corporate beliefs are primarily expressions of the solidarity of the community—the chairman, for instance, wrote that "believing is mainly belonging."[9] But the philosopher, Basil Mitchell, precisely reverses this relation and declares that "to belong to a church is to believe what the church believes."[10] Another member of the commission, John Bowker, a theologian who is also competent in information theory, seemed to be criticizing the sloppiness of much Anglican theology when he declared: "Information does not just slop around the universe in a random or arbitrary manner; it is channeled and protected, coded and organized."[11] Admittedly, doctrines are not adequately equated with "information." But it has always been held that they have some cognitive content, and to the extent that they do, one has to be concerned with their truth and internal consistency.

The report of 1981, therefore, more than its predecessor of five years earlier, tends to support Stephen Sykes' view that there is a definite Anglican doctrinal position. In a composite chapter written by three members of the commission, the bases of doctrine are spelled out more fully than had been done by Sykes. One of the writers describes what he calls "doctrine declared," that is to say, doctrine made explicit in written statements. He thinks of a kind of pyramid, with the Bible at the top, then the creeds, the articles, the Prayer Book, the ordinal, the canons, pronouncements of Lambeth conferences and, presumably a step lower, of the General Synod. Perhaps a place would have to be found too for documents like those produced by ARCIC on the eucharist, ministry and authority, for although these have not as yet been officially approved by the Church of England, still less by the whole Anglican communion, they are not simply the work of private theologians but of theologians officially appointed to represent the Anglican point of view. A second section of this chapter deals with "doctrine implicit," chiefly the doctrine that is implicit in the liturgy and in the way it is done. A final section entitled "doctrine diffused" reminds us that the history of the English Church has been so closely tied up with the general history of the English people that there is a kind of penumbra of doctrine continuing to subsist in "folk religion," and although this may be unsophisticated and may verge on mere superstition, it may be useful for the Church to be reminded of what people on the fringes *expect* churchpeople to believe.

Stephen Sykes also called for a more serious engagement with systematic theology among

Anglican theologians, and I have much sympathy myself with this view. I have said already that, properly understood, systematic theology does not freeze the issues. It always has an open and provisional character—this is true alike of Barth, Tillich and Rahner, to mention three recent practitioners—and in no way inhibits that theological freedom which is part of the Anglican heritage. The neglect of systematic theology among Anglicans is due in the main, I think, to a series of historical accidents. In the first place, the Reformation in England was much less radical than in countries that went the way of Calvinism and Lutheranism, and while we may be glad of this, since it preserved strong links with the catholic tradition, it did tend to produce a kind of theological lethargy. While in other countries that had been touched by the Reformation it was felt incumbent to produce confessions of faith and, very soon, textbooks of dogmatics, the Church of England believed itself to have abided by the faith of the universal Church. The articles of faith that it produced did not attempt a systematic statement of Christian theology as a whole, but only dealt with those matters where Anglicanism had broken with certain ideas that had prevailed in the medieval period. This already introduced that lack of proportion which we noted as characteristic of the 1938 report, *Doctrine in the Church of England*, where matters of ecclesiology receive far more space and attention than what one might consider the more fundamental doctrines of God, Christ and salvation. A second point is that the preoccupation with the Bible and the Fathers in Anglican theology has tended to stifle development and creativity. This is especially true since the rise of the critical historical method. As Sykes points out,[12] it has led to a type of theology that is parasitic, in the sense that it criticizes the tradition but makes no contribution of its own to what ought to be a growing, expanding tradition. To a large extent, we have to look to the continent for creative theology, for genuinely new Christian insights that seek to express the inherited truths in the thought-forms of our own time. Regrettably, one has got to admit that there is some truth in the old quip that theology is created in Europe, corrected in England and corrupted in the United States! This leaves to England the necessary but hardly exalted task of correcting the work of others. Even this task, it must be confessed, is often neglected, for Anglican theology tends to be somewhat insular, and one is often astonished in looking through the index of English theological works to note the almost complete neglect of continental theologians and philosophers who have had an influence on theology. To give an example, a collection of essays by Cambridge scholars on christology (of which, incidentally, Stephen Sykes was one of the editors),[13] made no mention at all of Rahner, in spite of his very important contributions to this subject! The only non-British theologian to get any coverage was Tillich, and that was in a chapter contributed by an American! This gives me the opportunity of saying that the final part of the quip which I quoted, about theology's being corrupted in the United States, is certainly not true today, if it ever was. American theology, just as much as European theology, has shown itself to be imaginative and constructive.

So far I have been talking about Anglican theology in general, and especially about the ways in which it has found expression in the liturgy and in various official doctrinal pronouncements of the Church. I would now like to turn our attention to the long line of individual Anglican theologians who have been writing in the past four centuries or thereby. They form a varied company, as indeed we might expect after what we have seen of the broad limits within which Anglican theology goes on, yet we can discern a kind of family resemblance among them.

Let us go back to Cranmer, perhaps the principal architect of the Reformation in England. His principal theological work, published in 1550, bears as its full title: *A Defence of the True and Catholic Doctrine of the Sacrament of the Body and Blood of our Saviour Christ: with a Confutation of Sundry Errors concerning the Same, Grounded and Established upon God's Holy Word, and Approved by the Consent of the most Ancient Doctors of the Church*. This very title tells us quite a lot. In the first place, it is no specifically Anglican doctrine that he intends to set forth, but "the true and catholic doctrine." In the second place, he intends to base himself on scripture, and secondarily on the Fathers of the Church, whose interpretation of the scriptures he hopes to show are supportive of his own. In the book itself, he enlarges his norms by including reason, claiming that in his teaching "nothing is spoken either contrary to holy scripture, or to natural reason, philosophy or experience, or against any old ancient author, or the primitive or catholic church; but only against the malignant and papistical church of Rome."[14] Here then already in Cranmer we have a clear statement of the basic characteristics of Anglican theology, which bases itself first on the scriptures, next on the teachings of the early Church and its doctors, and finally on reason and experience.

Still in the sixteenth century, an important work was that of John Jewel, who about 1560 wrote *An Apology of the Church of England*. The

most important part of this work is a defense of
the Church of England against the charge of
heresy. In successive sections, Jewel rehearses the
beliefs of the Church: "We believe that there is one
certain nature and divine power which we call
God . . ." He then speaks of the three persons of
the Trinity, then of the Church (not omitting "that
there be divers degrees of ministers in the church;
whereof some be deacons, some priests, some
bishops"), and goes on then to the sacraments,which, he says, are not "cold ceremonies,"
for "we affirm that Christ doth truly and presently
give his own self in the sacraments."[15] Jewel's
apology was directed mainly to defending the
Church of England against the attacks of Rome.
One of Jewel's pupils was Richard Hooker, whose
Laws of Ecclesiastical Polity appeared between
thirty and forty years after Jewel's *Apology*.
Hooker's defense of the Church was directed
more against the Puritans, and between them
these two early Anglican writers clearly marked
out the *via media* of the Church of England:
Catholic, in that she believed herself to continue
in all essentials the Church of the early centuries;
Reformed, in that she also thought it an obligation to rid herself of some of the doctrinal and
practical innovations that had come along in the
Middle Ages. But Hooker made it quite clear that
the Church is not frozen to the actual explicit
words of scripture. Tradition and reason were
assured of a place alongside scripture, though
subordinate to it.

Not for nothing has the epithet "judicious" been
applied to Richard Hooker. With admirable judgment, he held together on most matters the Anglican "troika" of scripture, tradition and reason. It
was inevitable, however, that this judicious balance would be lost by lesser men. Nevertheless, in

the century after Hooker, the type of theology that he had created remained dominant in Anglicanism. The seventeenth century was indeed the golden age of classical Anglicanism, the era of the Caroline divines such as Lancelot Andrewes, William Laud, Jeremy Taylor and others. According to historian John Moorman, it was their contribution that enabled the Church to rise again after the disasters of the Civil War and the Commonwealth. The attitude of this group is summed up in the last words of Bishop Thomas Ken: "I die in the holy catholic and apostolic faith, professed by the whole church before the disunion of east and west. More particularly, I die in the communion of the Church of England as it stands distinguished from all papal and puritan innovations, and as it adheres to the doctrine of the cross."[16] No doubt the Church of England has often been far removed from this lofty vision, yet one may claim that the ideal of the *via media*, a pure and primitive catholicism, fostered by these seventeenth-century divines, has never ceased to inspire the Anglican communion.

In the eighteenth century, the so-called Age of Reason, there was inevitably a swing toward rationalism. The extreme form of this rationalism was, of course, deism, and it was an Anglican priest, Matthew Tindal, who became one of the leaders of that school of thought. His book, with the self-explanatory title, *Christianity as Old as the Creation, or, The Gospel a Republication of the Religion of Nature* (1730) became virtually the "Bible" of deism. The deists were opposed by Joseph Butler, perhaps the greatest of all Anglican theologians, but the effectiveness of his opposition to deism was due in no small measure to the way in which he incorporated rationalism into his own theology. At the same time evangelicalism became

a force to reckon with. Its most famous represent-
atives, Wesley and Whitefield, clashed sharply
with Butler when the latter was Bishop of Bristol,
and eventually they passed out of the Church of
England. But a powerful evangelical influence remained, as did also a lingering residue of deism,
manifesting itself from time to time in the extreme liberalism of near-unitarianism of some far
out groups and individuals.

In the nineteenth century the Oxford Movement
tried to recapture the spirit of classical Anglicanism. Keble himself edited a new edition of the
works of Richard Hooker. Newman wrote elo-
quently of the *via media* and declared about the
formularies of the Church of England: "It is a
duty which we owe both to the catholic church
and to ourselves to take our reformed confessions
in the most catholic sense they will admit."[17] It
was surely a great tragedy for the Church of
England and for Anglican theology that he later
turned away from his early convictions. Pusey too
was reviving the traditional Anglican way of
theologizing. When a sermon of his on the eucharist was condemned by the university authorities at Oxford, he proceeded to show that his
teachings about the real presence and the eucharistic sacrifice were all derived from ancient
Christian authorities, in case, as he said, his
judges through ignorance might find themselves
condemning "St. Cyril of Alexandria, when they
thought they were only condemning me."[18]

There can be no doubt that the Oxford Movement did much toward reviving in the Church of
England an appreciation of the distinctive Anglican theological tradition, and this has been apparent both in official pronouncements of the
Church since the time of the Movement and in the
work of many individual theologians. But even in

the nineteenth century, it was already too late to restore the synthesis of the classical divines of the sixteenth and seventeenth centuries, even if that had been thought desirable. Anglicanism, like other Christian communions, including even that of Rome, has entered on a time of theological pluralism. Perhaps the most we can hope is that the authentic spirit of the *via media* will continue as a strong influence among the conflicting movements of the present time, ensuring the continuance of a Christian theology rooted in the biblical witness, true to the catholic tradition and commending itself by its inherent truth to reasonable men and women.

Chapter 3
The Anglican Liturgical Tradition

3

The Anglican Liturgical Tradition

by Marion J. Hatchett

THE PRINCIPLES upon which the first Book of
Common Prayer of 1549 was based were spelled
out in the order calling in the old service books
and in the Act of Uniformity for the first revision.[1]
These documents state that the first Book of Common Prayer was (1) "grounded upon the Holy
Scripture," (2) "agreeable to the order of the
primitive [i.e., early] church," (3) designed to be
unifying to the realm, and (4) designed for the
edification of the people.

"Grounded upon the Holy Scripture"

The documents cited state that the Book of
Common Prayer is "grounded upon the Holy
Scripture." Here is a Renaissance and Reformation emphasis. The Scriptures were newly available in the West in the original languages, and
they were being made accessible to the people in
the vernacular. Liturgical changes in the medieval
period had cut back substantially the amount of
Scripture read publicly. The lessons at the Eucharist had been reduced to two, and almost all of
them were taken from the New Testament.
Furthermore, they were reduced drastically in
length. For example, the 1928 Prayer Book had in
the little snippets appointed as Epistles from the
Sixth through the Twenty-fourth Sundays after

Trinity what remained of an earlier course reading of the entire corpus of Paul's epistles in their Biblical order. In the medieval period the eucharistic Psalms were also reduced to one or two verse snippets. The Daily Offices ceased being congregational and became the private devotions of the clergy, so the people were no longer exposed to the whole of the Scriptures read in course in the Offices, and the multiplication of saints' days so affected the Daily Offices that even the clergy were deprived of a substantial diet of Scripture. Less than two chapters, for example, was left of the old course reading of Isaiah in Advent. Rather than the rich variety of canticles of earlier rites, the medieval Roman eucharistic rite settled on one fixed canticle, the Gloria in excelsis.

Preaching became less and less frequent; some medieval reforming councils legislated that in every church there should be at least one sermon every year. Furthermore, sermons were not preached in the context of the Mass but of the Prone (the ancestor of the Protestant preaching service).

The late medieval books dropped many Biblical emphases found in earlier books. The early Roman books, for example, had a Proper Preface for every Mass; late medieval books contained only about a dozen. Or compare the late medieval Roman baptismal rite with earlier rites: the death-resurrection and birth imagery of the Scriptures and the earlier liturgies has largely dropped out, leaving the emphasis mostly upon baptism as a bath to wash away original sin.

Cranmer revised or deleted texts that he felt were contradictory to Scriptural teaching, but he did not take the view of many continental reformers that something must have Scriptural precedent to be admitted into the liturgy.

"Agreeable to the order of the primitive church"

The documents cited state that the Book of Common Prayer is "agreeable to the order of the primitive [i.e., early] church." Anglicanism looked to the early period of church history as normative. This period provided a means for interpreting Scripture, and a norm for doctrine, discipline, and worship. As one early Anglican bishop, Lancelot Andrewes, put it, Anglicans believe in one canon, two Testaments, three creeds, four church councils, and the church fathers of the first five centuries.[2]

We know a lot more about this normative period of church history than Thomas Cranmer could possibly have known. As a matter of fact Cranmer had no early liturgies available to him, no liturgical documents more than two or three hundred years old. He went through early sources that were available, sources such as the sermons and catechetical instructions and letters of the church fathers which were in print by that time, and made lists in his commonplace books of details about the liturgy of the early church that he could glean from such sources. He was that conscientious in his desire to recover for Anglicanism the liturgy of the early church.

He realized, for example, that the pattern of worship in the early church was daily Morning and Evening Prayer and Sunday and Holy Day Eucharists. He realized that the people participated actively in the liturgy rather than using it as a background for private devotions. In the late medieval period the ordination rites had become so elaborate that there was debate about what did constitute the sacramental sign; Cranmer realized that it was prayer with laying on of hands. He realized that at an earlier stage the Eucharist had contained a rich diet of canticles (not just Gloria in excelsis); that it contained substantial Psalmody and more and lengthier lessons from the Scriptures; that it contained a sermon and substantial intercessions; that the people offered the bread and wine; that the whole of the Eucharistic Prayer was said aloud, and that it contained thanksgiving for redemption and an epiclesis; that the Bread was broken into pieces for the Communions of the people, and that the people did receive Communion in both kinds within the rite, not individually and privately after having made a private confession.

While Cranmer could pick up from his sources many details about early liturgy, he could not learn about structures and the order of the elements.

Unifying to the Realm

Liturgical uniformity was not a part of medieval church life. Books were copied by hand, and they were revised in the process. No two churches had exactly the same liturgical texts. The pope was a conservative, so it would never have occurred to him to kneel to receive Communion, though some Westerners were beginning to receive kneeling. One or two candles were beginning to be found on altars. On festal days the priest wore the best vestments the church owned, and it did not matter whether those were black or white, or yellow, or blue, or brown. Immersion was the normal manner of baptizing, but pouring was becoming fashionable in some areas.

The documents cited state that the Book of Common Prayer was designed to unify the realm. Those in power in church and state hoped to bring together a heterogeneous group of people, and one of the means used would be the establishment of a uniform liturgy, something that would have been impossible prior to the invention of the printing press.

The Book of Common Prayer was designed to establish one *common* liturgy as opposed to the various regional or parochial uses. It was designed to establish a pattern of liturgical life *common* to clergy and laity alike; the Daily Offices were reestablished as liturgies for both clergy and laity, rather than as individual obligations of the clergy. This liturgy would also be one of the means used in the effort to establish English, the language of the city of London, as the language of the whole of the king's realm.

From a practical standpoint this establishment of uniformity was made easier and cheaper by pulling the various rites and directions that had been scattered through a number of volumes (missal, breviary, manuale, pontifical, and "pie") into one book which, with the Bible, would provide all the necessary texts and be within financial reach of parishes and of individuals.

Uniformity was made easier by the simplification of the rites. As the preface of the first Book of Common Prayer pointed out, in the late medieval rites, "many times, there was more business to find out what would be read, than to read it when it was found out." In the Prayer Book rules were "few in number" and "plain and easy to be understood."

Though there was to be uniformity in the texts used, in the interest of unity in a church and nation divided between those of the "old learning" and those of the "new learning," the use of ceremonies was left basically to the individual conscience (see, at the end of the first Prayer Book,

"Of Ceremonies, why some be abolished and some retained"), as was the continuation of certain practices, such as private confession (see the second exhortation in the eucharistic rite).

Edifying to the People

The documents cited state that the book was designed to be edifying to the people. In contrast to the medieval rites in an unknown tongue, with very infrequent preaching, which served the laity largely as a setting for private devotions, and which had begun to be interpreted allegorically, the rites of the new book were designed to be comprehensible, relevant, instructive, effective in building up the church and in establishing the people in godliness.

To this end the rites were to be in a language "understanded of the people." Morning and Evening Prayer were to be reestablished as congregational rites with the Old Testament read through each year, the Psalter every month, and the New Testament (except for Revelation) three times each year. Every Eucharist was to have a sermon or homily. Exhortations were interjected into the rites. A catechism was introduced for teaching purposes and as the initial portion of the confirmation rite. Baptisms, confirmations, and marriages were to be celebrated at public services. The most accurate translation of the Scriptures was to be used, and the rites were to be subject to revision or modernization (see the Preface and the section "Of Ceremonies").

Let us look now at the results of the application of these principles in the first Book of Common Prayer and in subsequent revisions.[3]

The 1549 Book of Common Prayer

The 1549 Book of Common Prayer presented a revised liturgical pattern for the observance of

the day, the week, and the year. Cranmer attempted to restore the pattern of the early church
of daily morning and evening services. The basic
content of his Daily Offices was the reading of the
Scriptures in course. He attempted to recover the
pattern of the liturgical week of the early church
with the Daily Offices culminating in the Sunday
and Major Holy Days Eucharist with Communions of the people. Wednesdays and Fridays, the
traditional station days, were to be marked by use
of the Litany. Cranmer greatly simplified the
Church Year, basically adopting that of the German Church Orders. (These were based on a false
assumption that days commemorating principal
New Testament saints were older than Black Letter Days.)

Since Cranmer had no early liturgies available
to him, what were his sources, and how did he use
them? Was the book, as some have said, simply
Sarum simplified, or was it, as others have suggested, simply another German Reformation
Church Order?[4]

Cranmer relied heavily on the writings of the
early church fathers that were available to him.
He made use of some Eastern liturgies that had
recently come into print in Latin, and of some
edition of an ancient Gallican rite. He used various medieval uses of the Roman rite, and the
reformed breviary of the Roman Cardinal Fran-
cisco Quiñones. He used several German Reformation Church Orders, especially the *Consultation* prepared by Martin Bucer for Hermann von
Wied, the reforming Archbishop of Cologne. He
used his own two earlier drafts for Daily Offices,
and various English Reformation formularies (reformed Primers, royal injunctions, the Bishops'
Book, the King's Book, the Rationale of Ceremonial, "Cranmer's Catechism," and the Book of
Homilies).

Let us look at the eucharistic rite as an illustration of how Cranmer used his various sources in his efforts to recover a liturgy Scriptural, Patristic, unifying, and edifying. In order to recover a richer use of canticles, Psalms, and lessons, and substantial intercessions, the Sunday Eucharist was always to be preceded by Morning Prayer and Litany as congregational rites. A full Psalm was substituted for the snippet that had been used as an introit. The Kyrie and Gloria in excelsis were to be said or sung straight through rather than in a farced or troped version. Some of the old collects of the day were replaced with new ones (for example, I and II Advent, Christmas, Quinquagesima, the First Day of Lent, I Lent, I and II Easter, the Sunday after Ascension, and most Saints' Days). Others were translated from German revisions or reworked to eliminate the intercession of saints and to stress the doctrine of justification by grace (for example, "that we may deserve to praise thy holy name" becomes "that we may worthily praise thy holy name"). Some Epistles and Gospels were lengthened. The Graduals, Alleluias, Tracts, and Sequences were omitted, possibly because they had sometimes covered some elements associated with the offertory. A sermon or homily was required. An exhortation, largely dependent upon German sources, was inserted. The bread and wine were to be furnished by the people, and to be placed on the altar just before the Sursum corda. The whole of the eucharistic prayer was to be said aloud. The Prayer for the Whole State of Christ's Church portion drew from both the Roman Canon and German Prayers of the People. The remainder of the prayer drew from the Roman Canon, the Greek Liturgy of St. Chrysostom (for the epiclesis), German and English Reformation formularies, and the writings of St. Basil. The amplified Institution Narrative of the Roman rite was replaced by one that was a conflation but that relied entirely upon the Scriptural narratives. Since in the late medieval period eucharistic piety had come to center on the elevation of the Elements at the Institution Narrative and Cranmer wished to recover a eucharistic piety centered on the receiving of the Sacrament, the elevations at the Institution Narrative that had been introduced in the late thirteenth and the fourteenth centuries were explicitly forbidden. Communion was preceded by an invitation, general confession, absolution, "comfortable words," and Prayer of Humble Access, taken largely from Hermann's *Consultation*. This preparation for Communion form had precedents in the late medieval devotions connected with the practice of receiving Communion from the reserved Sacrament immediately after private confession. For the medieval form "Behold the Lamb of God, who takes away the sins of the world" at the showing of the Elements to the people prior to Communion, Cranmer pointedly substituted a new text:

> Christ our Paschal Lamb is offered up for us, once for all, when he bare our sins on his body upon the cross, for he is the very Lamb of God that taketh away the sins of the world; wherefore let us keep a joyful and holy feast with the Lord.

The 1549 book specified that wafers be "without all manner of print, and something more larger and thicker" and that each "be divided in two pieces, at the least," thereby recovering the symbolism of Christ's body broken and of bread shared. The people were to receive the Cup as well as the Bread. The Sentences of Administration came from Lutheran sources ("given for thee"). Cranmer replaced the variable postcommunion prayers with one fixed prayer, and appended a blessing from the Lutheran tradition beginning "The peace of God which passeth all understanding."

The various sources were used in quite analogous manners in the other rites of the book. It is simply not true to say that the 1549 book was basically Sarum simplified, but neither is it true to say that it is simply another German Church Order. Though drawing from many sources, the book had its own integrity.

The 1552 Revision

From the early seventeenth century it has been popular in some Anglican circles to idolize the 1549 book, but that book was not well received at the time. It was too radical for the Devonshire rebels, for various conservative bishops such as Edmund Bonner, Thomas Thirlby, and Stephen Gardiner, and for priests who continued to use the old service books or to "counterfeit Masses." On the other hand, its revisions were not radical enough to satisfy the Norfolk rebels, or continental reformers who had come to positions of prominence in England, such as Martin Bucer and Peter Martyr, or the Anabaptists, or some of the clergy and bishops, such as John Hooper and John Knox.

Much has been written about the Protestantizing tendencies of the first revision of 1552, and there are quite a few. A penitential introduction was appended to the Daily Offices, for example, and Psalms were included as alternatives to the Gospel canticles. The preparation of the table at the offertory was dropped. The eucharistic prayer was abbreviated. Different Sentences of Administration were substituted, and the "Black Rubric" which denied "any real and essential presence" inserted. The exorcism and the chrismation were dropped from the baptismal rite. The burial rite was simplified, the eucharistic propers for burial dropped, and almost all petitions for the departed eliminated. References to the chasuble, the alb, the tunicle, and the cope, and to candles on the altar, were dropped. The giving of other instruments in addition to the Bible was eliminated from the ordination rites.

The 1552 revision certainly represented a move to make the book more acceptable to those more favorably inclined toward the continental reformation, but it also brought back various medieval elements in an effort to conciliate conservatives. For example, a few Black Letter Days were restored and a remnant of the octaves. The obligation to say the Daily Offices was laid on all clergy, not just those holding cures. The late medieval custom of having the Epistle read by the priest rather than by the clerk was restored. The stipulation that the bread and wine be furnished by the people was dropped. The custom that had won its way in some areas in the late medieval period of having the people kneel to receive Communion was made obligatory. The Athanasian Creed was to be said thirteen times a year rather than six. At various points the revisions of 1552 were reactionary rather than Protestant.

The Second Act of Uniformity, which enforced the use of this new book on and after All Saints' Day 1552, spoke of the old book as a "godly order" that needed reform only because of misinterpretations and because of doubts as to the manner of ministrations. That seems to be a pretty fair statement of the attitude of the revisers. Many of the changes were aimed at tightening rubrics and at stating explicitly what was implicit in the 1549 book. In opposition to the Anabaptists, for example, the 1552 baptismal rite incorporates a new bidding and a new prayer which state more explicitly than any text in the 1549 book the doctrine of baptismal regeneration. The change in the text associated with the post-baptismal signation and changes in the "confirmation" rite make more explicit the incorporation of the historic signation into baptism itself and the adoption of the new Renaissance-Reformation rite of "confirmation."[5] The 1549 book had attempted to center eucharistic piety on receiving the Sacrament rather than seeing it elevated; the only old ceremonial specifically forbidden was the elevations at the Institution Narrative. The 1552 book has the people receive the Sacrament at precisely that point in the eucharistic prayer. The 1549 book specified that wafers be "larger and thicker" and that each be broken; the 1552 book restored use of real leavened bread in accordance with the use of the first thousand years throughout the church and the continuous use of the Eastern churches.

The 1559 Revision

The 1552 Book of Common Prayer was in use less than a year when Edward VI died and Mary ascended the throne. She restored the old Sarum rite, and most of the clergy acquiesced, but several hundred clergy and laity fled to the continent. Some continued to use the 1552 book; those at Frankfurt revised it; those at Geneva, under the leadership of John Knox, substituted a liturgy based on that of John Calvin but incorporating some material from the 1552 book.[6]

Elizabeth, in 1559, restored the 1552 book with some revisions.[7] Though the committee empowered for the task was made up largely of returned continental refugees, the changes seem to have been aimed at conciliating those of more conservative leanings. The "Black Rubric" was deleted. The 1552 Sentences of Administration were prefaced by those of 1549. An "Ornaments Rubric" (subject to varying interpretations), restoring the vestments of "the Second Year of the Reign of King Edward the Sixth," was introduced. A new calendar issued in 1561 contained more than sixty Black Letter Days. In 1562 a metrical version of the Psalter (to which was appended a few hymns and metrical versions of the Creed, the Decalogue, the Lord's Prayer, the Veni Creator Spiritus, and some of the canticles) was authorized for use before and after services and sermons; this was a concession to those who were enthralled with the metrical psalmody of the Reformed Churches on the continent.

In 1563 a document was first printed that would later affect liturgical revisions, especially in Scotland and America, the Apostolic Constitutions. This document, now normally dated about 380 A.D., claimed to be the instructions of the apostles themselves regarding the organization, discipline, and worship of the church, and it included a number of liturgical texts and instructions. Given the concern for reestablishing the liturgy of the early church, it is intriguing to imagine how different the first Book of Common Prayer might have been if this document had been available to Thomas Cranmer.

The 1604 Revision

Early in Elizabeth's reign (1562), the Scots established as their liturgy the Book of Common Order, based on John Knox's Genevan Service Book. Dissatisfaction with the 1559 book grew among those most influenced by the continental Reformed Churches. The "Ornaments Rubric" proved unenforceable. Official liturgies issued for special days of prayer or thanksgiving looked more and more like the Genevan liturgies. Puritan versions or revisions of the Prayer Book were published and used surreptitiously. Near the end of Elizabeth's reign, in response to this activity, Richard Hooker wrote the fifth book of his *Ecclesiastical Polity*, which was a systematic defense of the Book of Common Prayer.

When James I came to the throne, Puritans presented him with the "Millenary Petition," which consisted largely of protests against features of the 1559 book. The Hampton Court Conference held shortly afterward authorized the making of a new translation of the Scriptures, the so-called King James Version published in 1611, and a slight revision of the Prayer Book that made a few concessions to the Puritans. The principal one was the revision of the provisions for private baptism to limit the ministration of that sacrament to the clergy. On the other hand, the Puritans were not altogether happy with the content of the addition to the catechism concerning the sacraments of Baptism and the Lord's Supper, and were offended by certain other minor changes such as additional Black Letter Days.

During the reigns of James I and Charles I a number of clergy came into positions of prominence and power (among them, John Overall, Lancelot Andrewes, William Laud, Matthew Wren, and John Cosin) who were anti-Calvinistic, concerned for "decency and order" in worship, and less negative than the Puritans about certain aspects of Roman, Lutheran, and Eastern theology and practice.

The 1637 Scottish Book of Common Prayer

As already mentioned, Scotland, instead of adopting the 1559 Prayer Book, had adopted a revised version of John Knox's Genevan Service Book, though this did not win its way throughout the land and eventually fell out of use in some of the places that had accepted it. The Scottish church in general retained or recovered certain elements lacking in the Book of Common Prayer (for example, a presentation of the bread and wine, an epiclesis, a Breaking of the Bread, and the liturgical use of "deacons"). The Scots were rightfully critical of the Book of Common Prayer as deficient in certain respects. On the other hand, they objected to the Black Letter Days, use of the Apocrypha, retention of the word "priest," and a number of other features of the English Prayer Book.

During the reign of James I episcopacy was established in Scotland and efforts begun to bring Scottish practice more into line with the Book of Common Prayer. Finally, in 1637, an effort was made to impose a revision of the Book of Common Prayer on the Church of Scotland.[8] This has often been referred to as "Laud's Liturgy," and was for many years thought to have been the work of Archbishop William Laud, for a copy of the revisions in Laud's handwriting was extant. It is now known, since the discovery of other manuscripts, to have been the work of Scottish bishops, principally John Maxwell and James Wedderburn, which was sent to Laud for his perusal, and from which he made a copy. The book incorporated a number of features valued by the Scots, such as a presentation of the elements, an epiclesis, a Breaking of the Bread, and the liturgical use of deacons. It downplayed the Apocrypha, substituted the word "presbyter" for "priest," used the King James Version rather than the Great Bible for Scriptural passages, and incorporated other changes designed to make the book more acceptable to the Scots. But other changes were made that were offensive to the Scots (for example, an increase in the number of Black Letter Days), and it was still entitled "Book of Common Prayer," and it retained the basic format and contents of the 1604 book, and bound with it to take the place of the beloved Scottish metrical Psalter was a new version, "The Psalms of King David as Translated by King James." Efforts to introduce this book brought a temporary end to episcopacy in Scotland.

The 1662 Revision

In England further struggle arose over the new Laudian canons of 1640, which legislated ceremonnial matters previously left to the individual conscience. In 1641 a committee of the House of Lords criticized certain Laudian innovations and recommended concessions that it hoped would appease the Puritans, but the move was too late and the concessions too few. The use of the Book of Common Prayer was outlawed, and in 1645 *A Directory for the Publique Worship of God* replaced it. About 3200 clergy lost or left their cures. This affected not quite thirty percent of the parishes.

The *Directory* was the result of compromise among several groups—Scots and English of presbyterian persuasion, some who adhered to free church principles, and some with moderate episcopal principles. The book provided rubrics and models rather than fixed texts and was fleshed out by different people with different forms: extemporaneous prayers, materials from the Scottish Calvinistic tradition, forms "in Scripture words" (such as Richard Baxter's), forms taken largely from or modeled after those of the Book of Common Prayer (for example, those of Robert Sanderson), or even material from Eastern liturgies (for example, the rites of Jeremy Taylor). In a few remote areas, in private chaplaincies, among exiles abroad, and in Virginia, the Book of Common Prayer continued in use. During the interregnum, Anthony Sparrow and Hamon L'Estrange published the first systematic commentaries on the Book of Common Prayer.

The restoration of the monarchy in 1660 had depended in part upon the promise of certain revisions and freedoms. The Puritans presented their "Exceptions" and Richard Baxter's alternative liturgy at the Savoy Conference, but by that time people anxious to restore the Book of Common Prayer were in control both in Convocation and in Parliament.[9] Cosin prepared a draft for revision, "The Durham Book," which made some concessions to the Puritans but was largely based on notes he and Wren had made earlier.[10] Relatively few of the recommendations of either the Laudians or the Puritans were incorporated in the 1662 revision. The occasional thanksgivings, more occasional prayers, and Bishop Sanderson's "Sea Forms" were added. Some changes were made in texts, including the insertion of a petition for the blessing of the water in the baptismal rite, a commemoration of the departed in the Prayer for the Whole State of Christ's Church, and a petition to deliver us from "privy conspiracy and rebellion" in the Litany (a slap at the Puritans). The most important changes were in the rubrics, and many of these came from the Scottish book of 1637 and represented a heightening of eucharistic doctrine: the bread and wine were to be presented at the offertory, the eucharistic prayer was given the title "Prayer of Consecration," the Breaking of the Bread was restored (though within the prayer), a portion of the eucharistic prayer was to be repeated over any additional elements needed for the Communions of the people, and consecrated Elements remaining were to be consumed by the communicants rather than being given to the curate for his own use. On the other hand, the Black Rubric was restored, but in a form that denied not "any real and essential presence" as in the 1552 book but "any Corporal Presence of Christ's natural Flesh and Blood." The ordination rites were tightened against presbyterian interpretation. The Epistles and Gospels were taken from the King James Version. As the result of the Act of Uniformity enforcing this revision about 1760 clergy, close to twenty percent, were ejected from their livings. The 1662 revision is still the official Prayer Book of the Church of England.

The 1789 Revision

Many of the proposals of Puritans, on the one hand, or Laudians, on the other, did not die with the passing of the Act of Uniformity.[11] Significant attempts at reconciliation were made through proposals for revision in 1668 and 1689. Early in the seventeenth century some Anglicans began to have great respect for Eastern liturgies, especially the Apostolic Constitutions, and to value certain features peculiar to the Prayer Books of 1549 and 1637 that seemed closer to the ancient and Eastern liturgies. Edward Stephens, William Whiston, John Henley, and others published and used with small groups liturgies based on these sources. Additional rites were bound with Prayer Books printed for use in Ireland. Non-jurors, unable to hold positions in the Church of England because of their adherence to the Stuart monarchy, reprinted the 1549 and 1637 eucharistic rites, and then in 1718 published some rites based on Eastern models. Thomas Deacon in 1734 published his *Compleat Collection of Devotions,* which he later used with his splinter group of Non-jurors. Scots Non-juring Episcopalians in 1722 issued the first of a series of "Wee Bookies," editions of the 1637 eucharistic rite, for use with the other rites of the 1662 book. One of the early Scots Non-jurors, Thomas Rattray, might be called the first Anglican liturgiologist, for he used the methods recently developed on the continent for scientific study of liturgy, and reconstructed the ancient Liturgy of St. James, which along with other ancient rites would affect the later revisions of the "Wee Bookies."

Early in the eighteenth century sentiment for revision arose among those of Latitudinarian sympathies who stressed reason and morality and were tolerant of variation in doctrine, government, and worship; numerous proposed revisions and arguments for revision were published. Three that were to contribute to the first American revision were *Free and Candid Disquisitions* (a collection of anonymous essays by different authors, edited anonymously by John Jones of Alconbury and published in 1749), *The Expediency and Necessity of Revising and Improving the Publick Liturgy* (another anonymous 1749 publication, to which was appended a proposed revision, *A New Liturgy*), and *Reasons Humbly Offered for Composing a New Set of Articles of Religion* (published anonymously in 1751 with twenty-one specimen articles). Eighteenth-century forerunners of Unitarians, the so-called "Arians," also published revisions. Several of these took as their starting point a Prayer Book amended by Samuel Clarke, whose Christology was censured by Convocation early in the century. The most influential of these "Arian" revisions were those edited by Theophilus Lindsey, for a chapel he set up after leaving the Church of England over the issue of subscription to the Articles of Religion. Benjamin Franklin collaborated with Sir Francis Dashwood in an "Abridgement" of the Prayer Book published in London in 1773. This revision was more radical than the title would suggest; symbolic of the "abridgements" was the abridgment of the Gloria Patri to one word, "Amen." In 1784 John Wesley published a revised Prayer Book for American Methodists, and in 1785 King's Chapel, Boston, adopted a revision based on that of Theophilus Lindsey. Persons who were to exercise leadership in the first revision of the Prayer Book for the American Church were familiar with and sympathetic to these various revisions.

The possibility of a revision that would find general acceptance was complicated not only by liturgical and theological issues but also by political and personal enmities. As the only hope of unity seemed to lie in making just those changes necessitated by political independence, the first interstate convention adopted this stance as a "fundamental principle." In August 1785 Bishop Samuel Seabury and a committee appointed by him proposed revisions for Connecticut that followed Latitudinarian lines; these were sent on to Boston for a convention of other New England states. That convention added other proposals and forwarded them to a convention of states south of New England scheduled for late September in Philadelphia. A Virginia convention and a number of prominent individuals sent additional proposals. As a result, the states meeting in Philadelphia set aside the "fundamental principle" and authorized a revision for trial use.

Seabury, when he saw how unpopular his first proposals were with the conservative church people of his diocese, did a sudden about-face and set himself against the Proposed Book, denouncing it months before the first copy came off the press. All the state conventions except Connecticut and New Jersey authorized trial use of the Proposed Book, and it served as the basis for the first American Book of Common Prayer authorized by the first General Convention of 1789.

The Proposed Book updated the language slightly, simplified the rules on fasting, eliminated Black Letter Days from the calendar and readings from the Apocrypha from the lectionary, omitted the Ornaments Rubric, cut back on repetitions in various rites, substituted "presbyter" or "minister" for "priest," omitted the Black Rubric, abbreviated somewhat various pastoral offices, revised the baptismal rite to downplay original sin and baptismal regeneration, edited and abridged the Psalter, and appended an abridged version of the Tate and Brady metrical Psalter and a selection of hymns. It omitted the phrase "He descended into hell" from the Apostles' Creed and omitted the Nicene and Athanasian Creeds altogether. Many of these changes had been recommended in the documents that had come to the Philadelphia convention from the various states, and most of them had a long history in the revisions and proposals of various schools of thought. Within weeks of the publication of the book the state conventions of both Maryland and Pennsylvania, states in which the Scottish eucharistic prayer had been used, recommended the revision of the eucharistic prayer to incorporate a portion of the Scottish prayer, and Samuel Parker, rector of Trinity, Boston, wrote in favor of adopting the Scottish prayer. Weeks later Seabury published a revision of the Scottish Communion Office and in September 1786 recommended its adoption in Connecticut, though, according to Ebenezer Dibblee, one of the Connecticut clergy, it was "with *a noble spirit rejected*" by the clergy of Connecticut. In October an interstate meeting in Wilmington, Delaware, recommended the restoration of the deleted phrase to the Apostles' Creed and the restoration of the Nicene Creed as an alternative to the Apostles'.

When the first General Convention met in 1789 it authorized a revision of the Prayer Book based on the Proposed Book of 1786. Some of the elements were restored from the 1662 revision, and other texts and changes were brought in from various proposals of the period. In certain respects the 1789 book was more conservative than the Proposed Book. The most important restorations were the use of the word "priest," though it was not restored in every place in which it had been used in the 1662 book; bringing the baptismal rite back closer to that of 1662; and including the whole Psalter and the whole Tate and Brady metrical Psalter. On the other hand, despite the Wilmington Convention of 1786, the omission of the phrase "He descended into hell" from the Apostles' Creed, or the substitution of another phrase, was allowed. The revision was more radical than the Proposed Book in that it allowed omission of the Trinity Sunday Proper Preface, deleted the references to private confession in the Exhortation and in the Visitation of the Sick, abridged the Benedictus Dominus Deus, and omitted the Magnificat and Nunc dimittis, and in various other respects. The most important feature of this revision was the eucharistic prayer modeled after that of the Scottish "Wee Bookies," which was closer to the historic eucharistic prayers than those of the 1662 book or the Proposed Book. It

has often been said that this was based on
Seabury's Communion Office, which had been
based on the 1764 "Wee Bookie," but a comparison of the texts will show that it contains phrases
from earlier versions of that prayer that had not
been retained in the "Wee Bookie" of 1764 or in
Seabury's revision of it. It was this earlier form of
the prayer, probably that of the "Wee Bookie" of
1755, which had been used in parishes in Maryland and Pennsylvania and had been the basis for
the recommendation of the 1786 Maryland and
Pennsylvania state conventions.

The 1892 Revision

The 1789 revision was contemporaneous with
the French Revolution. The fright which this revolution created brought in a period of reaction, of
looking to the past for models, of antiquarianism,
of romanticism. The supposed order and stability
of the Middle Ages and of the classical eras of
Greece and Rome began to have a great appeal. It
issued in neo-classic and neo-Gothic architecture,
romantic music and poetry, and the Gothic novel.
In Anglicanism there was a revival and consolidation of old-fashioned high churchmanship, evidenced in such writings as those of William Jones
of Nayland in England, and of Bishops John
Henry Hobart of New York and Theodore Dehon
of South Carolina in America. This came at the
time of a gradual loss of fire among Anglican
evangelicals, a reaction in some circles against
Calvinism, and a growing boredom with Puritan
plainness. Anglicans were further frightened by
the multiplication of denominations, the tolera-
tion of Romanism in England, and the wave of
Roman immigration to America. All of this
worked together to set the stage for the Oxford

and Cambridge movements which attempted to emphasize or reclaim the Anglican Catholic heritage. Medieval rationales were used to interpret Prayer Book rites (see, for example, the late-nineteenth-century efforts to reinterpret confirmation). Medieval rites were reprinted and studied. Hymns from the medieval Latin repertoire and plainchant settings of canticles and service music came into use. Neo-Gothic began to be thought of as the only proper church architecture, and churches were built or remodeled according to ideals conceived by the Cambridge Ecclesiologists, which despite their intentions had little relationship to the arrangements or uses made of the buildings in the medieval period. Attempts were made to recover medieval vesture and ceremonial and color sequences, and here, too, it was often Baroque Roman vesture and ceremonial and color sequences, that were adopted, under the assumption that what Roman Catholics were wearing and doing in the nineteenth century was medieval in origin. Controversies about "ritualism" broke out in every province of Anglicanism.

In England, despite many proposals for Prayer Book revision, the political controversies and the strife within the church were such that the only successful revisions were the dropping in 1859 of the old "State Services" to commemorate the Gunpowder Treason Plot, the Martyrdom of King Charles, and the Restoration of the Monarchy, and a revision in 1871 of the lectionary for the Daily Offices. In Ireland the Prayer Book was revised in 1877, with some concessions to evangelicals and some tightening against the growing "ritualism" of the period and against certain "advanced" interpretations of the rites. In this country, on the other hand, under the leadership of William Reed Huntington, who proposed the Chicago Quadrilateral, a process of Prayer Book revision was begun in 1880 in the interest of "liturgical enrichment and increased flexibility of use" that would culminate in the very conservative revision of 1892.[12]

The 1892 revision did provide many enrichments. The Apocrypha and Revelation were included in the Daily Office lectionary, and alternative readings were provided for Lent, the Ember Days, and the Rogation Days. The Gospel canticles were restored to the Daily Offices. The Kyrie was restored to the eucharistic rite. A Penitential Office was provided for Ash Wednesday. Propers were appointed for the Feast of the Transfiguration.

This revision also allowed more flexibility, chiefly in the interest of shortening services. The Decalogue, the Exhortation, and the penitential introduction to the Daily Offices could now be used less frequently. The eucharistic rite could be abbreviated when used for Communion of the Sick. To take the place of Morning and Evening Prayer with special propers, a briefer burial office was provided. But one of the new freedoms would have disastrous effects upon the normal Sunday morning liturgy and upon the liturgies for certain special days. Previous Prayer Books required that on Sunday Morning Prayer be followed by the Litany and at least the Ante-Communion if not the whole of the eucharistic rite. This kept the people aware that we were a church not of Word or Sacrament but of Word and Sacrament. Prior to 1892 the only circumstance in which the Prayer Book allowed a celebration of the Eucharist that was not immediately preceded by Morning Prayer was for a private Communion of the Sick. The Sunday morning liturgy was lengthy, and it contained a great deal of duplication. There was both the Litany and the Prayer for the Whole State of Christ's Church, for example, and the Lord's Prayer was said at least three times. The service began with confession of the sins committed since last coming to church, but before approaching the Table one had to confess the sins committed since the beginning of the morning service. The 1892 revisers, rather than allowing for omission of duplicatory material, allowed Sunday Morning Prayer without Ante-Communion and allowed the Eucharist not preceded by Morning Prayer. Parishes were caught choosing between Word and Sacrament; some said the Eucharist is so important that it must be celebrated every Sunday at the principal service at the expense of the Word, while others said the Word is so important that we must use Morning Prayer as the principal service with great frequency at the expense of the Sacrament. This also affected very adversely the liturgies for special days. The old readings for Morning Prayer on Easter from Exodus and Romans were replaced by resurrection passages. The tension of the Palm Sunday rite with Morning Prayer setting forth the entry into Jerusalem (with the crowd crying "Hosanna" as they greeted one whom they expected to show himself as a political Messiah) in contrast to the eucharistic lections (in which the crowd cries "Crucify" and Christ shows himself as a Messiah who reigns from a cross) was lost as churches scheduled not Morning Prayer and Eucharist but either Morning Prayer or Eucharist. For these and other reasons I would be willing to argue that the 1892 revision has been the worst revision in Prayer Book history.

The 1928 Revision

Many of the recommendations for the 1892 revision not accepted at that time gradually found favor. The years immediately before and after that revision saw the church begin to accept many of the enrichments desired by the "ritualists" and to become more tolerant of other peoples' use of other enrichments. These years also saw the rise of the Social Gospel and Liberal Protestantism. As early as 1913, General Convention took the first steps toward revision of the 1892 book. The early decades of this century were also a time of tremendous advances in liturgical scholarship, including the reconstruction of the third century liturgy of Hippolytus, the Apostolic Tradition, but few American Episcopalians were aware of these advances, and they played little part in the revision of 1928. That revision was still primarily concerned with enrichment and flexibility, as were Prayer Book revisions for Canada (1922), Ireland (1927), England (1928), and Scotland (1912 and 1929). The Daily Office lectionary was arranged in 1928 according to the Church Year rather than the calendar year. Additional prayers that expressed social concern were added. But in response to Liberal Protestant pressures Biblical typology was deleted from the baptismal and marriage rites. On the other hand, a number of additions and changes were made in response to the growing Catholic segment of the church. A rubric commending a "special confession" was restored in the Visitation of the Sick, and provisions were made for anointing or laying on of hands. Propers were provided for the Eucharist at a marriage and at a burial. The two most controversial changes were the restoration of prayers for the departed and rearrangement of the eucharistic rite so that the Eucharistic Prayer would flow directly from the Sursum corda through the people's Amen and the people's Communions would be preceded by the Lord's Prayer and the Prayer of Humble Access. Both were interpreted as Romish innovations by many, especially the latter, which smacked of eucharistic adoration.[13]

The 1979 Revision

The 1928 General Convention set up a Standing Liturgical Commission, one of the primary purposes of which was to prepare for Prayer Book revision. The 1928 book came at the end of an era. The beginning of World War I marked in Europe the end of an age of Romanticism, Neo-Gothicism, Liberal Protestantism, and rabid denominationalism. It marked the beginning of a new or renewed emphasis on Biblical theology, Patristics, and ecumenism, and of historical-critical study of liturgy, renewed lay participation with a rediscovery of the corporate nature of the church and the role of the laity, and different directions in iconography and architecture. Between the two World Wars a new Liturgical Movement began to spread among Roman Catholics in Germany, Belgium, Austria, Holland, and France, and to affect continental Protestantism and Eastern Orthodoxy. It was not until the late 1930s that it began to have some effect upon Anglicans, through the writings of Father Gabriel Hebert, Dean William Palmer Ladd, and Dr. Walter Lowrie. Its first fruits were the "Parish Communion" established in some places, the restoration of baptisms to public services, and increased emphasis upon congregational singing. Despite these trends, the Prayer Book revision proposals in the 1950s were principally concerned with enrichment and flexibility. In the 1950s, however, there was a gradual awakening to new directions within Romanism (particularly through early writings of Louis Bouyer and Josef A. Jungmann) and within continental Protestantism (especially Taizé), and to the new liturgy of the Church of South India. The Lambeth

Conference 1958 acknowledged that time had come for more drastic Prayer Book revisions and set forth guidelines that were more fully developed by the Anglican Congress of 1963. From that point liturgical revision in Anglicanism entered a new phase. The 1964 General Convention instructed the Standing Liturgical Commission to bring concrete proposals to the next convention. Twelve years of trial use, 1967–1979, culminated in the new revision adopted at the 1979 convention.[14]

No previous single revision has ever incorporated as many new texts or made as many changes as this one, yet it is firmly based on the principles that were spelled out in regard to the first Prayer Book of 1549: it is grounded on Scripture, agreeable to the practice of the early church, unifying, and edifying.

It is grounded on Scripture. Many Biblical emphases have been recovered; for example, the Biblical meaning of Sunday as the day of Creation, Resurrection, the outpouring of the Holy Spirit, and the foretaste of the eschaton. The Biblical typology has been restored to the baptismal rite. There is a renewed emphasis on the Holy Spirit, and an enriched doctrine of the church. And the Sunday congregation is exposed to the bulk of the Scriptures over a three-year period.

It is agreeable to the practice of the early church. The seven Eucharistic Prayers new to the book proclaim God as Creator and give thanks for the incarnation as well as the crucifixion. They proclaim the resurrection and point to the messianic banquet as well as recalling the Last Supper, and the epiclesis of these prayers is truly traditional rather than receptionistic. The primacy of Sunday is recovered, and the baptismal nature of the Church Year. The various orders of ministers—lay persons, bishops, priests, and deacons—

perform liturgically the roles that signify their functions in the Christian community. The liturgical pattern of Daily Offices and Sunday and Holy Day Eucharists is spelled out more explicitly. Various practices from the life of the early church have been recovered: reservation of the Eucharist for those unable to be present at a public service and for the Good Friday Communions; proper liturgies for special days; An Order of Worship for the Evening, the Noonday Office, and Compline; the exchange of the peace; standing as the normal posture for the Eucharistic Prayer and for the receiving of Communion; the implication in rubrics that real bread will be used; restoration of the relationship between baptism and church year, congregation, and bishop; recovery of use of chrism at baptism; Black Letter Days; joining together prayer with the laying on of hands at ordinations; sacramental rites for the reconciliation of a penitent; a principal Sunday liturgy that is a liturgy of both Word and Sacrament.

This new revision is unifying. It has been salve to the consciences of many scrupulous clergy who have wanted to be law-abiding as well as pastoral. It has done a lot to lay to rest some of the outmoded churchmanship battles of the past. Not only has it been a unifying factor within our own province of Anglicanism, but also it has brought us closer liturgically to Roman Catholics and to Protestants who have been affected by the Liturgical Movement. Many of the translations of canticles and other common forms are, or soon will be, in use in most English-speaking denominations. The eucharistic lectionary is a refinement of that now in use by Roman Catholics and by a number of Protestant communions. One of the Eucharistic Prayers was drafted by an ecumenical committee that included Roman Catholics, Lutherans,

Presbyterians, and Methodists, as well as Episcopalians, and is now approved for use in several
denominations.

The new revision stresses edification: an
enlarged eucharistic lectionary; lectionaries for
pastoral offices and encouragement of preaching
at pastoral offices and Daily Offices; expansion of
the catechism; strengthening of the rite of "Confirmation, Reception, and Reaffirmation of Baptismal Vows" as a rite for mature public affirmation;
provision of the regular rites, pastoral offices, and
Episcopal Services in contemporary language;
ceremonial enrichments; Proper Liturgies for
Special Days; flexibility in the Daily Offices and
other services, and the provision of so-called "Rite
Threes" for Eucharist, Marriage, and Burial.

The 1979 book is possibly the most drastic revision in Prayer Book history, but it is true to, is, in
fact, a further realization of, the principles—that
it be grounded on Scripture, agreeable to the
practice of the early church, unifying, and edifying—that underlay the first Book of Common
Prayer, the principles that define the Anglican liturgical tradition.

Chapter 4
The Anglican
Spiritual Tradition

4

The Anglican Spiritual Tradition

by Martin Thornton

THERE IS good reason for dividing this lecture into two unequal parts. I must first offer a brief resumé of what I take the Anglican spiritual tradition to be; then I should like to look rather more fully at the contemporary impact of our tradition, concluding with the somewhat dangerous game of attempting to read the signs of its future unfolding.

Pedantic haggling over the meaning of words is not the most exciting exercise, but it is apparent already that some attention must be given to that most ambiguous and abused term "Tradition": *parádosis, traditio*, literally a giving-over, or handing-over. Handing-*over* be it noted and not handing-*down*.

To the Fathers of the primitive Church, Tradition was almost synonymous with Revelation; it consisted of the saving acts of God in Christ—the incarnation, passion, resurrection and ascension—in other words in the Creeds to come, which were "handed-over" to successive generations. To be traditional was to be consistent with Divine Revelation: and this still pertains. Tradition is defined as "the continuous stream of explanation and elucidation of the primitive faith." To Bishop Francis White it is "derived from the Apostolical times by a successive current." Hundreds of additional references could be added, and many with the paramount simile of the river, as "stream" and "current" in those given above. Tradition, then is a living stream, a flowing river, and not a stagnant pool; it is something that moves. Tradition should never be confused, as it often is, with antiquarian nostalgia.

Neither should tradition be confused with custom. Visitors to England may have discovered the tradition whereby the crown jewels are displayed in the Tower of London guarded by the Yeoman dressed in Tudor uniform and armed with pikes. But the Yeoman of the Guard are customary; the real tradition is carried on by a plain-clothed cop sitting in the corner with a gun.

"Anglican" spirituality is often confused with, and even confined to, that which issued from the teaching of the Caroline Divines—which is why I prefer the adjective "English," despite its insinuation of insularity.

Nevertheless, for elucidation of this tradition, the seventeenth century is a good starting point, not because it is the beginning but because it forms a fulcrum; a point from which we can look back as well as forward. And this precisely because it is the Caroline method; they began by looking back to the New Testament and patristic roots, yet it was a golden age of future expectation. Anglicanism ever refutes the notion that it is a *sui generis* seventeenth-century invention, but rather that it is the result of continuous historical development. The seventeenth century may indeed be seen as the first full flowering of our tradition; a glorious new bloom that, like any pure breed, is derived by careful selection and cross-fertilization. Anglicanism has a pedigree going back to the New Testament, a spiritual lineage derived from the accumulated wisdom of the past.

What are the constituents of this pedigree? I have tried to trace it in some detail in my *English Spirituality*; here it must suffice to take a fleeting glimpse at four main areas.

(1) The first Christian millennium was largely dominated by the formulation of theology, and of liturgy in which it found expression. Following John Macquarrie, theology may be defined as the Church reflecting upon and clarifying its experience. It is significant that the Caroline Divines were so especially concerned with this period of creedal formulation, and outstandingly learned in patristic theology from both East and West. But the key Anglican authorities were, and still are, St. Augustine and St. Benedict.

(2) St. Bernard of Clairvaux dramatically changed the emphasis, initiating an upsurge of affective devotion of a largely personal kind, centered upon the living reality of the Sacred Humanity of Jesus. Devotion to the Blessed Virgin, and extra-liturgical cultus centered on specific aspects of the Passion, followed logically. A sane and disciplined emotionalism entered into Christian prayer.

(3) The absolute heart of the English-Anglican tradition is a constant attempt to synthesize these two poles: intellectual and affective, reason and emotion, corporate and personal, the head and the heart. And so if its Patriarchal founders are St. Augustine and St. Benedict, with a still living influence from St. Bernard, the more immediate father-founder of Anglicanism might be seen in the tremendously significant figure of St. Anselm. Thereafter influence is exerted by the later Cistercians, the School of St. Victor in Paris, the Canons Regular of St. Augustine, the Friars Minor, and the Thomist, rather than the Rhineland side of the Dominican movement.

(4) So to the universally acknowledged "English" School of the fourteenth century, embodying as perfectly as may be, this intellectual-affective, theology-devotion synthesis. The *Revelations* of Juliana of Norwich is probably the best example, and almost certainly the best known of all the fourteenth-century writings. It is a disturbingly vivid expression of affective devotion to the Sacred Humanity of Jesus; some would say veering toward feminine hysteria. But that is to miss the deep underlying current of trinitarian, christological and atonement theology that underpins each paragraph.

If this is the most obvious popular expression of the ideal its supportive ascetical direction is to be found in Walter Hilton's *Scale of Perfection.* Published in 1494 it continued to be reprinted up to 1679. The strong suggestion is that it continued to be the English clergy's *Vade Mecum* throughout and beyond the Reformation period. Legislation can be brought to bear on liturgy, ritual and ecclesiastical polity; social and political upheaval can change the superficial face of the Church overnight, but deep-seated personal devotion is less tractable. The transference from the medieval Latin Mass to Cranmer's first Prayer Book took one week, but it is unlikely that the Englishman's prayers changed all that radically from the first to the third of June 1549. Neither is it likely that English spirituality became suddenly Puritanical in 1552. It is more than likely that the influence of Hilton survived throughout.

And so to the fulcrum and watershed of the seventeenth century; the consolidation of a millennium of development. What are the fundamental characteristics of this germinal School of Prayer? There are again four distinguishing factors.

(1) The synthesis of theology and devotion, heart and head, sublimely achieved in the fourteenth century, remained the ideal: "true piety with sound learning"—"with" not "and"!—became the Caroline motto. But in an age of theological re-formation, of a searching for the primitive tradition, and with radical liturgical revision, it was almost inevitable that the theological head took precedence over the devotional heart. And I suggest that this situation is still with us; the Anglican ideal remains but not wholly fulfilled. Our history since the Caroline age, or more strictly since the fourteenth century, has been made up of attempts at the ideal only partially achieved by a series of swings of the pendulum. Like the Carolines we are still over-intellectual, suspicious of religious experience, unhappy with "enthusiasm," a little frightened of the human emotions. Caroline thought degenerated into Deism, the Evangelical revival of the Wesleys restored the balance, further rationalist reaction was countered by the Oxford Movement, which may have achieved the balance better than anyone since Juliana and Hilton: true piety with sound learning. But was its piety founded on the wrong model?

(2) The second integral Anglican characteristic is its insistence on the unity of the Church. In the Caroline period there was no gulf between priest and layman, no screened-off division between the sanctuary and the nave. There is another irony in that the doctrine of the Church was central to both Reformation and Oxford Movement, yet the Caroline ideal has never quite been achieved since: except, possibly, today.

Corollary to this emphasis was a deeply *domestic* spirituality; foreshadowed in the twelfth century by the glorious, and so English, foundation of St. Gilbert of Sempringham, and typified five centuries later by Nicholas Ferrar's Little Gidding. But it was the fourteenth-century English writers who invented the subtle and deeply significant term "homely": Margery Kempe enjoyed "homely dalliance with the Lord"; Juliana's "homeliness" hints at Baptismal incorporation into the Sacred Humanity, therefore habitual, constant, stable, and in the deep, contemplative sense, simple. Homeliness points to that form of contemplative prayer wherein one is united to God through a harmony with his creation; it has links with the recapitulation theory of St. Irenaeus, with the method of Hugh of St. Victor, and it is strongly developed in Juliana.

Less technically, the idea spills over into Caroline devotion as more down-to-earth domesticity; the source and setting for Christian life and Christian prayer is the village, the farm and above all the home, not the oratory or shrine: it is a Benedictine ideal. Of all the classical analogies describing the Catholic Church, Anglican spirituality favors the "Family of God": *Onward Christian Soldiers* is an eccentric deviation from Anglican hymnody.

(3) Symbolic of this emphasis on the unity of the Church, with its domestic spirituality, is the extraordinary weight of authority given by the Caroline Fathers to the Book of Common Prayer, from 1549 onward, and further up to 1928. It is customary for Benedictines to read selections from the *Rule* at silent meals, the Ignatian exercises still form the heart of Jesuit spirituality; but no school of prayer has been so firmly tied to a book as the Caroline Church of England. "Bible and Prayer Book" were the twin pillars of this spirituality, with the latter given almost equal status, and subjected to the same kind of systematic study as

the former. The Book of Common Prayer was subjected to annotation and commentary with not a rubric, colon or comma regarded as insignificant.

It is again necessary to look at the historical setting, for the Book of Common Prayer is derived from a long line of ancestors, ultimately from the Benedictine *Regula,* with which, ascetically, it has much in common: both are designed to regulate the total life of a community, centered on the Divine Office, the Mass, and continuous devotion as daily, domestic life unfolds. Both are concerned with common, even "family" prayer. Neither are missals, breviaries or lay manuals, because here the priest-lay division does not apply: they are common prayer, prayer for the united Church or community.

The vital principle, tragically missed by both modern liturgists and their critics, is that, like the *Regula,* the Book of Common Prayer is not a list of Church services but an ascetical system for Christian living in all of its minutiae.

To the seventeenth—or indeed nineteenth—century layman the Prayer Book was not a shiny volume to be borrowed from a church shelf on entering and carefully replaced on leaving. It was a beloved and battered personal possession, a lifelong companion and guide, to be carried from church to kitchen, to parlor, to bedside table; equally adaptable for liturgy, personal devotion, and family prayer: the symbol of a domestic spirituality—full homely divinitie.

(4) From all of this there emerges a Moral Theology of much originality. The majority of Caroline casuists—for that is what they all were—advocated auricular confession, but the emphasis changed from the application of juristic rules to the training of the individual conscience, toward moral maturity and personal responsibility. Caro-

line Anglicanism is Christianity for adults. This moral theology was not calculated by clerical professors in the universities; it was hammered out in the pulpit. And it was domesticated: the juristic distinction between "mortal" and "venial" sin became a pastoral difference between sins of malice and of infirmity; grace was the loving power of a present Redeemer, never mind the hair-splitting distinction.

I began by defining *tradition* as that which *moves*; it is not antiquarian nostalgia, but a synthesis of past, present and future; a flowing river not a stagnant pool. Tradition has its source, its roots, in the past, but it continues to develop and re-form (never forget that what happened to Anglicanism in the sixteenth century was not so much reformation but re-formation). Tradition begins with the present and looks both ways; to the wisdom of the past and to future development.

So what of the present? What of the future? What are the signs of an unfolding tradition? Prophecy is a risky business, but there are *four* factors that might be worth looking at:

(1) I have pointed to the central Anglican ideal, traceable at least to the teachings of St. Anselm, and perfectly expressed in the fourteenth-century English School: the head-heart, speculative-affective synthesis; true piety and sound learning. And we have seen how, while upholding that ideal, the Caroline period never quite got in balance; seventeenth-century spirituality was weighted on the intellectual side, at the expense of a proper emotionalism. Despite the Wesleyan reversal, and a brave attempt at righting the balance by pastoral Tractarianism, the over emphasis on the intellect, with a consequent fear of feeling, has characterized Anglican spirituality ever since.

The last two decades have witnessed three very significant signs of reaction, inevitably over-reaction, but given time, given a little more theological underpinning, something to be welcomed.

(a) The 1960s saw the rise of the "Jesus people." The Jesus kids to whom the established Church was too dull and respectable by half; to whom the liturgy was formal and lifeless; to whom theology was metaphysical and meaningless. But did they love Jesus! The movement seems to be waning but it should not be dismissed as simply a sentimental bit of childish playacting. While scholars were arguing about the historical Jesus and the Christ of faith; about the historicity of the saving acts of a demythologized gospel: the kids were loving Jesus, and they claimed experience of him in daily life. They were not so far from the Wesleys' "Christ as personal Saviour," and possibly a bit nearer still to the Cistercian reformers: the Patron Saint of the Jesus kids has to be St. Bernard. The 1960 brand of this classical spirituality may be dismissed as naive, brash, adolescent, shallow and immature, but if cultural factors have an ascetical impact, we cannot dismiss *Jesus Christ Superstar* or *Godspell* as impious. And it is not entirely without significance that contemporary Christology—the real scholarly stuff—has a good deal in common with those Jesus kids of twenty years ago: in their different ways, both are saying never mind the Chalcedonian categories, where is the whole, real, resurrected and ascended Lord: the Man-Jesus.

(b) If the Jesus kids rediscovered the real live Jesus, the Charismatics (or Pentecostals or whatever we call this total movement) claim to have rediscovered, or rather to have been rediscovered by, the Holy Spirit. It is difficult to believe, like Elijah to the priests of Baal (1 Kings 18.27), that the Holy Spirit has been asleep for four centuries. It is equally difficult to refute that something quite startling has happened, worldwide and ecumenically, in recent years. Could it be that the Spirit has indeed been active all this time but that the English-Anglican terror of religious experience has failed to respond? But the patient and long-suffering God always wins in the end, so perhaps latterly he has insisted on being heard and received. Such divine breakthrough is apt to cause explosive trouble in a sinful Church, and so there are facets of Pentecostalism that are disturbing and that look very much like heresy; for this the all too stolid Anglican of the past, fearful of the Spirit's activity, must take a good deal of the blame. If you persist in damming the river you are going to get a flood. Yet Pentecostalism is capable of theological interpretation, and things are settling down. Perhaps the pendulum swung too far, but it is returning to its balanced midpoint; to the head-heart synthesis. Now we have less fear of religious experience, of feeling and emotion; our exaggerated intellectualism is being softened as we return to our true ideal. The present revived cultus of Juliana of Norwich is very significant indeed. Sometimes awkward and embarrassing, but the Charismatics have done Anglican spirituality no mean service.

(c) Caroline theology made much of the Greek tradition. Hooker, Cosin and Beveridge abound in references to Athanasius, Basil, Chrysostom and the Cappadocians. But they stuck with theology. A significantly new Anglican movement is a rapidly growing interest in Eastern Orthodox liturgy and spirituality, with its wide range of experience from the simplicity of the Jesus Prayer to a profound creation-mysticism.

These three factors militate against that seventeenth-century tension, fear of experience and exaggerated distrust of the emotions, and so help to restore the doctrine-prayer, head-heart syntheses of true Anglicanism.

(2) That vague and diffuse philosophical stance which is generally known as existentialism is as much a product of sociology as of philosophy; it attempts to describe how modern people think rather than to produce an academic philosophical system, concluding that the contemporary interest is in existence, or experience, rather than in substance. The traditional creeds and formulae upon which spirituality is based are couched in substantive terms, which now need translating into existential terms.

To employ a simple analogy I have used elsewhere, to any modern person a knife would immediately be defined as something you cut things with. St. Athanasius would define a knife as metal. The latter is substantive thought: what it is composed of. The former is existential thought: what is it for, or how is it experienced; so without ever having heard of Kierkegaard or Sartre, modern people are existentialists.

Modern theology attempts to translate the old substantive categories—what are God's attributes, how are divinity and humanity united in Christ's person—into existential terms: how is God experienced? how do we confront the living Christ in the world? Back to the Jesus kids. And this too affects prayer, again by countering the over-intellectualism of the Anglican past and taking a sane but courageous view of religious experience. In personal devotion and liturgy, the substantive view issued naturally in discursive meditation and an insistence on understanding.

The existential view looks toward contemplative experience. All of which is added support to a return to the speculative-affective synthesis.

(3) We have noted that the unity of the Church is a basic characteristic of the Anglican spiritual tradition. The Church is one, welded together by the Book of Common Prayer, which will have nothing to do with priesthood as sacerdotal caste divorced and differentiated from the laity. Nevertheless this ideal also has not been constantly achieved. The eighteenth century divided priest and layman in terms of social status; the nineteenth century, under the influence of the Tractarians, returned to the medieval pattern.

The Liturgical Movement has the closest connection with the two previous points. In its present form it seeks to express a united family of God, in existential or experiential worship. The Central altar, the Westward position, increased lay participation, the liturgical Pax, all point in this direction. There is a certain fear of change, a certain criticism, especially in modern biblical language, and, like the charismatic and/or pentecostal upsurge, the pendulum could have swung too far. But the reaction is a healthy one, against Caroline tension, against deistic rationalism, against artificiality. Yet contemporary liturgy is "traditional" in a way that 1662 is not: it is based on a much profounder liturgical theology, a more respectful and scholarly attitude to the primitive—the English eucharistic rite is now based firmly on Hippolytus, 1662 is based on Cranmer! All of which is very good Anglicanism indeed!

(4) Closely connected with this point (3) is a return to lay participation, not merely in liturgical or administrative aspects, but in the deepest realms of prayer, of ascetical theology, of spiritual direction and of pastoral counsel based on the

Gospel (in my own English diocese of Truro the number of lay, and predominantly female, theology graduates is quite extraordinary and wonderfully welcome).

But this raises a problem of *authority* that is most pertinent to the Anglican tradition. It is well enough known that the English seventeenth century produced a galaxy of lay theologians: Henry Dodwell, Izaak Walton, Robert Boyle, Sir Thomas Browne, Susanna Hopton, Mary Caning, to name but a few of the most prominent. The tradition continues into this century: Dorothy Sayers, Lorna Kendall, and those with a more pronounced American flavor: T. S. Eliot, W. H. Auden, Dr. Dora Chaplin, and doubtless many more of whom I am unaware. But in the seventeenth century such names of repute were supported by a national network of lesser known but efficient laity.

The seventeenth century English parish was run by that remarkable partnership of parson and squire, sometimes in loving partnership, sometimes in envious rivalry, co-operating and squabbling alternatively. And yet it was generally understood that if the parson had a general oversight of the spiritual welfare of his flock, the squire had responsibilities for the pastoral care of his household; his family, his servants and his tenants. The squire presided at family prayers, which were based on the Prayer Book offices. His wife and adult daughters visited the sick, distributed alms and cared for spiritual development, according to their capacity, which was often more than competent.

This was the pastoral expression of the one united Church, with no great divide between priest and laity, and with every educated layman and laywoman accepting that serious pastoral responsibility which is happily returning. But the structure of Caroline society was such that social position and proven competence carried their own authority. Today we are bedeviled by qualification mania: diploma-itis. Up to around the mid-nineteenth century the qualification for a job—any job from spiritual direction to extracting bad teeth—was one's ability to do it; now one has to have a piece of paper signifying that you ought to be able to do the job but probably can't.

Today the Anglican Church has numbers of laity who are wholly competent in spiritual direction and other seriously theological pastoral skills. Very occasionally those to whom they could minister are wrongfully doubtful of their real ability: where is the magic bit of paper? Much more often the lay experts, who humbly know that they can do the job, hold back in anxiety over their authority: they have no bit of paper.

Modern Anglicanism has a straight choice in this matter: it can return to the Caroline ideal of One Church, one Christian community, of glorious diversity and spiritual talent; of uninhibited spiritual family talents, father supporting mother, son helping daughter, daughter guiding her brothers, and nephews and nieces joining in: to hell with the bureaucratic, qualifying bits of paper.

Or we can opt for the modern, and curiously also medieval, system of an authorized hierarchy: degrees in theology, diplomas in sociology, licentiates in pastoral counseling, *et al.* Or, medieval-wise, ordination to the office of deacon, sub-deacon, sub-sub-lay deacon, lector, doorkeeper, sacristan, server, cellarer (I rather go for that one), *et al.* The medievals meet modern America, contracted from the Germans, in diploma-mania. Now Western Europe, not least England, have caught the disease.

But the Anglican ideal cuts across all this nonsense. Can you, by the gifts God has given you—and please do not commit the blasphemous sin of pretending that he has given you none—help, support, guide and encourage your brothers and sisters in Christ to deeper devotion, adoring worship, creative prayer, redemptive sacrifice; the unleashing of the power of Christ. If you can, or think you can, or by grace you might: for God's sake get on with it. Never mind the bits of paper.

(I am terribly proud of being a Doctor of Sacred Theology of the General Seminary in New York, but I don't think I will mention it before the judgment seat of Christ.)

But we must be practical: We do live in a diploma-manic age. The other side of the coin is that we don't want quacks. At home we have courses in ascetics, in spiritual direction, and our Bishop publishes the names of those who have taken (taken not passed) such courses. This seems a good way out of the present dilemma.

Perhaps a creative synthesis will emerge, as Anglicanism has so often produced in the past—the developing, unfolding, *tradition*. Our ultimate value is that we believe in God not in ourselves. *Via Media* has nothing whatever to do with compromise; it has everything to do with spiritual sanity.

Chapter 5
The Oxford Movement
and Its Historian

The Oxford Movement and Its Historian

by Owen Chadwick

THE NAME is much less accidental than the name Oxford Group for a modern religious movement, which appears to have gained its nickname because its leader toured South Africa with some Oxford undergraduates and a porter chalked the words Oxford Group on the luggage. The name Oxford Movement was slower to develop. The first general name for the people was Tractites (1834) because they wrote tracts not liked by their critics. They called themselves Apostolicals, and the name came within a short distance of catching on. A later authority with a name for being untrustworthy alleged that at first they were sometimes known as Keble-ites, because Mr. Keble of Oriel College, professor of poetry in the university, was one leader; but this is incredible, I have found the name nowhere else, if anyone ever called them Keble-ites, it cannot have happened before 1864 and after that must have been very donnish. Next (1836) they were called Malignants, in an emotional tirade by Dr. Arnold of Rugby, also from Oriel College. Next year (1837) the same headmaster called them Newmanites, perhaps because Mr. Newman of Oriel supplied a lot of the ideas. Then in 1838 they were Puseyites—indeed it is alleged that this name appeared in common parlance three or four years before but we only seem to have written proof from 1838—because

Dr. Pusey formerly of Oriel, now a Canon of Christ Church and Professor of Hebrew, was an associate. Then they were Tractarians (1839), or Tractators (1842), or Newmanians, or Neomanians, Newmaniacs. The normal phrase became the Tractarian Movement, and this lasted until the end of the 1870s. If the phrase 'Oxford Movement' was used, the writer put it into inverted commas. The first book to narrate its history called it dryly, 'The Theological Movement of 1833'. But already in 1841 we find the first use, controversially, of the phrase 'The Oxford Movement'. At first it was associated with a partial meaning; here is a religious movement going on with various centers, Mr. Hugh James Rose for example in Cambridge or Dr. Hook in Leeds, and the Oxford part of it is the Oxford Movement. But already in the late 1840s, we have the word *Oxfordism*, a body of doctrine or an attitude so that, in the end, even Mr. Rose, though a very Cambridge man, could be said to be part of it.

In 1856 a vehement Roman Catholic called Browne, with the patronage of sixteen Irish bishops, wrote the first book called *A History of the Tractarian Movement*, which begins with the delightful sentence 'The progress of Christianity in England presents many curious features,' continues in the same vein, and was dismissed by Newman with the single word *trashy*, which is an exact description. He used the phrase 'Oxford Movement' in the text, but only in inverted commas. Even in the middle 1880s the phrase Oxford Movement was as often as not put into inverted commas by journalists. By then it had lost its immediate link with the university; and about the same time (first instance known to me 1878[1]) it began to be called the Catholic Revival by those who liked and afterwards the neo-Catholic Revival by those who disliked.

During the only part of my early education when I had a vestigial connection with the University of Oxford, I read Richard Church, *The Oxford Movement*; first published in 1891. It bowled me over. I thought it a wonderful book; such a lovely English style, such penetrating and yet amused understanding of human beings, such a poetic insight into the universe, such personal modesty and lack of ostentation on the part of the author, such a humane interpretation of the Anglican tradition in the context of the Catholic inheritance. When I put the book down finally, I revered Richard Church. I first learned to like Newman because Church admired Newman, and anyone whom Church admired must be most admirable. I thought Oriel the best of all Colleges, in the University of Oxford; not because Provost Eveleigh and Provost Copleston developed a system which attracted good men from other Colleges into the Fellowships; not because it produced in a single generation two men who won their way into the Anglican calendar of saints and another for whom exists a strong movement trying to insert him into the Roman Catholic calendar of saints; and a fourth who was the subject of a recent motion wishing to put him into the calendar of saints—an astounding record for any single college over centuries, and all in one generation—for none of these reasons did I revere Oriel in those days, but because Richard Church was a Fellow. I was sure that the book was a classic of historical literature.

That it is a classic of literature no one can challenge. That it is a classic of *historical* literature, that is in question. Decades after the first reading hesitations and scruples crept in; and

102 / The Anglican Tradition

those hesitations and scruples affect the interpretation of the Oxford Movement. Geoffrey Best has beautifully put some of these hesitations in his introduction to the more recent edition of the book (London, 1970).

Everyone knows of cases where a book is so important in forming opinion and yet is bad. *Eminent Victorians* is not just a bad book, it appalls. Yet its non-historical quality is such that even now we can hardly understand Dr. Arnold or Cardinal Manning aright because Lytton Strachey's portrait is stamped upon their faces as a magic indelible dye. Is it possible that this book by Church is the opposite of a bad book that blinds—namely a book so good that it blinds? Does Lytton Strachey take worldly masks and fit them upon characters that were in part though only in part otherworldly? Does Church take otherworldly masks and fit them on characters that were in part, but only in part men of this world as well as of another? Is he the literary equivalent of the artist George Richmond, who painted the loveliest pictures of the Victorians and painted them all with a farseeing refined spirituality in their faces; the aesthetic antidote to Lytton Strachey?

I am now going to ask in turn two questions about this classic history of the Oxford Movement, two questions that sound as though they must be contradictory and yet are not; first, why is the book so excellent? Second, why is it a failure?

Why is it excellent? Three reasons, in order: form, matter, range. Church adopted a particular literary form, the essay. He was one of the best essayists in all the Victorian age, that great age of essay-writing. In those days intelligent journals could make good profits out of selling (what by modern standards would be) very few copies; and therefore catered for an elite public who would tolerate in one number an article of thirty, forty or even at times a hundred pages; so that intelligent magazines drew writers out of the ordinary because they could shade their journalism into something more satisfying.

Church once explained why this mode of communication attracted. The professional scholar writes for an enclosed world. He is shackled by sources, criticism of text, defense of argument, constraint on personal opinion, weight brought by striving toward completeness. The essayist says what he thinks. The reader wants to know about the man or matter of which the author writes, but is happier still to know what the author feels. He is free; bringing readers into his confidence, able to follow wherever taste or interest selects, careless that his pages may be ephemeral provided that he stirs others to read about his concern. He once talked of the need to throw off the *donnishness* of erudition (*Misc. Essays*, 1, 4). (The earliest instance of the word *donnishness* to mean a stiff pedantic manner is found a few years before in Church's own colleague and leader Newman). Something about the idea of the word *essay* contrasted in Church's mind with the word *pedantry*; unbuttoned instead of stiff, human instead of arid, using knowledge instead of massing information, outgoing instead of jealous, loving knowledge with an affection that must wish to share its insight, bridging the chasm between an older society and our own by letting each be part of the other, men of former generations understood to be of the same blood and sinew and heart as ourselves, ourselves able to share their fears and hopes and emotions. He looked for breadth because he had a sense that narrowness was blind, because breadth could compare and so illuminate, because intense specialization grows stale and if the purpose is to understand humanity and society freshness of mind is an indispensable quality in the inquirer— breadth of freedom or humanity contrasted in his mind with a cramped and servile assiduity (*Misc. Essays*, 1, 5).

So here is great essayist, who can write English prose as fair as Newman's, who is readable because he eschewed of set purpose the foot-slogging of the professional historian, and who thinks it right to take the reader into his private confidence. From this aspect, at least, the Oxford Movement was fortunate to have its historian in a man who was no journalist, in any wrongful sense, but whose account is hard to put down.

The next reason for the quality of the interpretation is range. Some people took very simple views of the why of the Oxford Movement. They said dismissively, it was a part of the European right-wing reaction after the French Revolution; and its origin was in political theory. Or they said, it was the ecclesiastical reaction against the Reform Act and the new representative system in Britain; and its origins lay in politics, a war against the Irish Church Temporalities bill. Or they said, it was the recovery of old Arminian teaching in an age when the evangelical revival made Calvinism so loud and so intrusive; and its origins lay in controversial theology, a counter to Calvinism. Or they said, it was only the religious side of the Romantic Revival, and we must set it with Wordsworth's poetry and Walter Scott's novels—a harking back to the past, a release to the imagination—and its origin lay in the new sensibility about history.

Political theory, politics, ecclesiastical reaction, anti-Calvinism, romantic imagination—all were contemporary diagnoses, and all had more than a breath of truth. But Church had a range to see that no contemporary diagnosis was sufficient. To understand this religious movement we must set it in a far longer context. Its intellectual base lay in a tradition framed in Richard Hooker, or Lancelot Andrewes, or Jeremy Taylor, the English divinity of the seventeenth century; and beyond them to their roots, the hard and rigorous study of the Fathers during the age of the later Reformation. It was the recovery of perspective. It was the setting of the Church in the length and breadth of the Christian centuries. It was a lifting of the eyes to Christian horizons. It was a taking of older truths or insights out of the cupboard, dusting them, and seeing almost with surprise that they mattered. And this mattering was not just intellectual, was not primarily intellectual. It made a difference to religion, and to moral attitudes.

This was the second reason for Church's quality. He had range. He had written the best book on Lancelot Andrewes, the best book on Dante. He understood, not just the Victorian age, but the Christian centuries. He had the indispensable perspective.

The third reason why the book is so good is the subject. It had everything that a great historical subject should have: unity of theme; limits of time, set close; fascinating and strange characters, some of them noble; a sense of inspiration, and leaping vitality; a war; and a tragedy.

Church was fascinated by people. He never lost sight of richness and variety, and yet the ordinariness of human beings. The secret of this sense was the refusal to despise. Men and women when they are different—and if they are in the past they are always different—do deeds that look to later generations bizarre; the easiest and the least understanding form of historical writing is veiled satire or veiled mockery. To refuse to despise is not to refuse to laugh. Men are what they are and sometimes they are tragic and sometimes they are comic but in either case they are often laughable. The quest for humanity has to rest upon a sense of the seriousness of the object, that is, an attributing of some sort of lasting value to the person or group that is being studied. It did not depend on the moral philosophers with their analysis of human nature in the abstract; even though an elementary knowledge of moral philosophy could not but be useful to the student of man. But in Church's eyes the student of man was always the student of men, living individuals; and he felt this study of the being in its various specimens to be stranger and more wonderful and more curious than the abstractions of humanity offered by students of will or of conscience or of aesthetics of beauty (cf. *Misc. Essays*, 1, 7).

Nineteen chapters to a book on the Oxford Movement, and two of the chapters are on lesser men—Isaac Williams and Charles Marriott. Why? Can it be said that either contributed anything to the ideas or even the history of the movement, except in so far as by Dr. Pusey's folly Williams was beaten to succeed Keble in the professorship of poetry? We hear that Williams was a great cricketer—what is that to do with us? What is to do with us is that this is a convert of John Keble; a poet; a quite unostentatious curate; reflecting Keble; reverent; humble; unambitious; with a horror of display; the very type of what the Oxford Movement professed. We hear that Marriott could almost distress his hearers by his clumsiness to say what he meant, his long looks and blank silences; we hear how he wore a black veil over his college cap and that in his rooms you must make your way between layers of books—what has that to do with us? Because this quaint eccentric lovable *character* was Newman's devoted, almost dog-like, disciple, who carried out most of the textual drudgery for the schemes of making the early Christian Fathers known.

We meet the leaders through their disciples; and somehow Keble and Newman are the more enchanting when we see their reflections. Contemptuous of the world and its praise; scholarly, but not for scholarship as an end in itself, scholarship to bring us the Christian past and so help us morally; reserved, their religion the opposite of the religion of the market square; self-disciplined; with strong sacramental life and a longing to recover the glory of the sacrament for the Churches; never frightened of being dull, preferring restraint to excitement; at times odd, at times remote, but the more otherworldly for their remoteness and the more interesting for their oddities.

A part of the subject made fascination: its tragedy. The movement could not hold its leader. Twenty years before Newman wrote a charming book about his own desertion of the Movement and how that calamity happened. Church had no need to repeat. But throughout Church's book lurks a sense of tragedy, at times a grim tragedy. You would have expected the story of a man who found peace and happiness in a new church to be the opposite of a tragedy. Church found in it nothing but tragedy. I am going to put it to you that this makes part of the failure of the book. But here I put it as a constituent of its stature. It is a piece of history to engage in emotions, and that is not so common in the study of the past, wherein we watch frightfulness with mild indifference.

Now I will ask, what is wrong? Here is a man with every possible gift for writing the history of the Oxford Movement and he failed. How could that be?

In the incomplete book, published by his daughter and son-in-law, is a historical obsession. This *thing* within the book may very likely have caused him hesitation before he printed. It is an onslaught upon the heads of Oxford College, taken corporately.

Everyone knows that heads of colleges are not the most popular persons in a university. Everyone knows that they are the butts of academic politics, and will later appear in ludicrous lights among many memoirs. But this is no acidulated don. Never was a Victorian less brash. This is one of the most humane and refined minds of the nineteenth century. And he is not a disappointed man, with the motives of a Mark Pattison of Lincoln College for being sour. He is successful in the rightest sense of that double word. He is mellow, and comfortable, and kindly, and humorous, and wise, the best kind of Victorian gentleman. What demon bit him that he should insert into his book long passages that remind one of the shadier controversies of modern academic warfare?

The needle of one's twenties and thirties becomes a dagger in one's sixties and seventies. As the long memory gets longer it grows clearer and more indignant, till a man may find that he *harbors* rancor. What went wrong? The Heads of Oxford Colleges, that was what went wrong. They drove Newman out. They behaved with unexampled unwisdom; and worse than unwisdom, he tells us, they were childish, they failed, and failed deplorably, in justice and in charity; they were blind to the moral quality before them because they were incapable of seeing moral quality— 'There was that before them which it was to their discredit that they did not see' (p. 262). They were violent, and ignorant (p. 263), they wanted learning, they were scandalous in their imputations of dishonesty, they were 'inexpressibly childish' in sticking up notices at the gates of the schools or in college butteries. The whole affair was a 'continuous provocation of unfair and harsh dealing from persons who were scarcely entitled to be severe judges' (p. 270); all held up by Church to a contrast with the noblest motto ever possessed by a university: *Dominus illuminatio mea.* In short, two chapters at least of the book are not history but a philippic; an old man, whose bitterness had been repressed in his middle years, coming out at last in the long perspective of the last years before death.

When men denounce the heads of the Colleges with fury, they mean, when you boil it down, the Head of their own College. Hawkins, the provost of Oriel, was an intelligent man. Church confessed his stature. He was able and resolute. He was a man 'of rigid conscientiousness, and very genuine though undemonstrative piety, of great kindliness in private life' (p. 283). But he had not 'breadth' or 'knowledge proportionate to his intellectual power'. And that means he was incapable of understanding what Newman and his friends stood for.

This is Church's view. Everyone is agreed that Hawkins was the weightiest enemy of the Oxford Movement in all Oxford. Hawkins is strange. Liddon thought him a very able theologian. He could be a good talker at dinner. Everyone is agreed that he was a good man, a man of conscientiousness. But in Oriel he was nicknamed the East Wind.

They said that he was *sharp*. Never did a man see so many trees and so little of the wood. He was exact about everything that was small. An undergraduate drank too much and fell off the roof and died; and the provost took a long time to arrive, and when he appeared his tie had been tied perfectly. He was a master of detail, and cold to get detail right. He could not see what all the details were for. (See Burgon, *Lives of Twelve Good Men*, 225–29, 238.) 'He would have set a King right,' said one of the bishops, 'if His Majesty had slipped in a date.' Therefore he had the highest dislike and disdain for the Oxford Movement, whether on its moral or its intellectual side. And so Church can sum it all up in a fearful condemnation: 'In their dullness of apprehension and forethought, the authorities of the university let pass the great opportunity of their age' (p. 215).

A young man went up to Oxford as an undergraduate. The time was exciting in the university. He started attending the sermons at St. Mary's given by a Fellow of his own college at 4 p.m. on Sundays. They were not well attended, because the delivery was not inspiring and the preacher held an ideal of sobriety that made him eschew those of the lesser arts that made words interesting. There in his pew at St. Mary's the young Church was soon enchained by the moral force of the preacher, his insight into conscience, his sternness with the waverer, his compassion for the tempted, his *burning*[2] faith in God and His counsels.

And then this religious leader, to whom he owed his soul, deserted the cause. What devastation! What destruction, not only of the cause in Oxford University. Newman's leaving meant the exploding into laughter or contempt of some of the noblest religious idealism that the Church of England had ever seen. And incidentally it caused agony to disciple after disciple—what were they supposed to do now? Join him in Rome, whose teaching they could not believe? Abandon the ideals that they learnt from his lips? Mark Pattison looked back upon that moment with gratitude, as if he were released from thraldom of mind, delivered from a nightmare, brought out suddenly from the darkness of obscurantism into light. The going of Newman, said Pattison, was like the opening of the shutters in the chapter of a sick man who has slept till midday (Pattison, *Memoirs*, 1969 ed., 189, 236, 238).

At that moment of time Church was a little closer to Newman even than Pattison. What was he supposed to do? Join Newman? Give up his ideals? Recognize that this new idea of the Anglican Church was all illusion?

Some of Newman's disciples were like Pattison, willing to blame Newman for their predicament. But not Church. His former leader was too noble, too sincere, too honorable. He would say no word against him. Nevertheless, the obsession against the heads of colleges who drove out Newman had its roots here. He could not believe that Newman went because he chose. He went because he was driven. For Church the heads of colleges became a scapegoat, which bore away the blame, and so rescued the integrity and honor of his former leader, and enabled him to retain his own convictions.

Then why should he write at all? He was being forced to write a book that ends not only in a public calamity but a private misery. What forced him to such work which might be fascinating but was certainly unpalatable? One of the reasons for the failure rests here; at least half of the author did not want to finish the book. To finish the book was pain.

A very central doctrine of the Oxford Movement is the doctrine of reserve. Hide the self. Give excellent lectures on poetry if you can but give them in Latin so that no one will be tempted to come for mere enjoyment. Preach in such a way as to make yourself small, not so as to make hearers think you are a good preacher. Read prayers unemotionally, lest your personality intrude. Try not to have your portrait painted. Do not write an autobiography. Newman wrote half an autobiography but then he had been libeled. We cannot imagine Keble or Pusey writing an autobiography.

Church's history of the Oxford Movement is not an autobiography. But if you read it carefully you see that at times it is a little too near autobiography for comfort. These events changed his own life; were explosive in his own career. The emotion can still be felt.

Old men may brood about the tragedy of their youths, but usually they cannot bear to publish; and this man was a Tractarian, a friend of Newman, a disciple of Keble, whose religious ideal contained self-restraint, and not pushing the self, and quietness, and being reserved. There must be some other cause, besides the long secret resentment at injustice and blindness. Such a man would only publish, would only dream of publishing, if he saw a need—that is, something had to be corrected. An impression, propagated, printed, accepted, assumed, spread wide, was unhistorical and being unhistorical hurt Christianity, hurt the Church of England, hurt his friends, hurt his own inmost soul. He had to amend.

So the next question is, what is it that so urgently needs reminding that it forces the most

Tractarian men to behave with so unTractarian a ferocity?

The answer is clear. It was, first, Tom Mozley, and secondly, Mrs. Hawkins.

The 1880s was the age of the Reminiscences. The young ardent men who sat at Newman's feet in the Oxford of the 1830s were born a few years after the century, and by 1880 were in their seventies or more. They had therefore reached the age when the mind ceases to reach forward, but turns backward to illuminate the past, which now becomes very sharp to the memory. So they began to reach into their memories: Mozley, Mark Pattison, Burgon, James Anthony Froude the historian and younger brother of Hurrell Froude.

Now the doctrine of reserve produced a peculiar and perhaps harmful result. The people who owed their souls to the Oxford Movement and still felt grateful and loyal, said nothing. The people who owed their soul to the Oxford Movement and then reacted against it, and now criticized or even hated it, said plenty.

Tom Mozley wrote his *Reminiscenses of Oriel College and the Oxford Movement* during 1881, finished it by November, and published it in the spring of 1882.

No one could have a better qualification; far better than Pattison, rather better even than Church. Undergraduate at Oriel, then Fellow and intimate of Newman; he often dined with Newman, sometimes breakfasted with him of a morning, often walked with him of an afternoon; Newman felt an affectionate friendship for him. Mozley sat on the original committee that planned the *Tracts for the Times*; helped to distribute those Tracts in Northamptonshire and Derbyshire, though he was accused of being a bit idle in the campaign; was strong on Newman's side in the battle against the Provost of Oriel; assisted him at the sacrament, stood in as his curate; and sealed all this intimacy in July 1836 by marrying Newman's sister Harriett. Newman admired and honored him at that moment beyond anyone else. 'I know no one of a higher and more generous mind—and unless it was throwing words away in these common place days to say so, of such heroic qualities—I mean I think him possessed of the most affectionate heart, and that he would do anything, neglect himself, and go through all perils for those who are possessed of it. Everyone who knows him at all must and does know this in a measure and though my words seem high flown, yet they are very true.'[3] From Newman, Tom Mozley took the editorship of the Tractarian journal *The British Critic*.

And now came the cloud between these two intimates and brothers-in-law. Mozley took Harriett on a visit to Normandy and was bowled over by the worship in the Roman Catholic churches which he entered. He found it far nearer to the ideals he had learnt from Newman than the prosy readings which he associated with the Book of Common Prayer. He decided that he must be a Roman Catholic. Newman hurried down to the Oriel living of Cholderton to stop him, and persuaded him to undertake to make no move for two years. Harriett Mozley was shocked by all this and broke off relations with her brother. The parting of friends had begun.

Therefore from 1843 they could no longer be intimates, though their hearts were not finally sundered for another four years. But from 1833 to 1843 they held nothing back from each other. Newman once said, as he looked over his old letters, that the letters from him to Tom Mozley, and from Tom Mozley to him, made the history of the movement to Rome and of his own change.[4]

Tom Mozley became a writer of leaders for the *Times*. In his old age he claimed to have written 10,000 leaders. Experts in the history of the press tell me that this is impossible, but it could have been several thousands. That practiced his pen but hardly endeared him to Newman, for to be a reporter on any newspaper, *Times* or not, was regarded by middle-class early Victorians, and not only by churchmen, as equal to a lapse into the criminal classes. He seemed to have deserted his high ideals, and taken up work unsuitable for a clergyman, and secular in tone. And now, 1882, he published his reminiscences; and like Pattison an ex-disciple, with the acidity of an ex-disciple. He wrote to old Newman before the book was published to say how he was sure that not a line in the book would pain Newman (Mozley to Newman, October 20, 1881)[5]. Newman sent him back a friendly little warning against being caustic.

The warning was needed.

When the book appeared, it was well received at the first flush of enthusiasm. Some good minds thought that he penetrated, as none before him, the inwardness of the Oxford Movement. Pattison praised it to the skies, but then Mark Pattison wanted the Oxford Movement to be despised. 'It is the one book,' wrote Pattison, 'to which, next to and as a corrective of, the *Apologia pro Vita Sua* the future historian of Tractarianism must resort.' And from Pattison, the doctrine was taken up by the *Dictionary of National Biography* (s.v. 'T. M. Mozley') and so consecrated. One of Newman's sisters liked it very much. The *Times* liked it, but the *Times* is apt to like books written by its employees. Nearly everyone else thought it deplorable.

Newman was horrified. He read a few pages and could read no more. 'Chapter 2 has so knocked me down.' It was full of mistakes. 'All that you have said,' he told Tom Mozley, 'is so uncalled for that I am almost stupefied.' He thought it cruel and untrue about his father. Mozley 'is a wild beast who rends one's hand when put up to defend one's face' (Newman to F. W. Newman, June 13, 1882). 'When a man aims at gossip,' he told Pusey, 'he is obliged to dress up facts in order to make his story stand upright.' 'Very ill-natured' he called it to another friend. He resented it that some people seemed to read it with pleasure, and amusement, and even thought that they understood the Oxford Movement better in consequence. 'Wanton mistakes' he told Copeland. After his first protest, he never wrote again to Tom Mozley though characteristically he was very kind to Mozley's only child when, not two days before his death, she came to visit him at the Oratory.[6]

Was all this fury justified? Mozley's eyesight was bad. He could not check anything. He had a mass of old letters but he could heardly read them. He wrote two volumes out of his memory. The memory of the old is notorious. Inaccuracies sprouted on page after page. He never saw proofs. Longman's printed straight from his manuscript. Everything about the book shouted the epithet unscholarly and gossipy.

Never did so many people write letters to the newspapers proving or claiming that this or that was untrue. But Newman had a special reason for hating the book. He could not bear the world to know two facts about his father; first that his bank failed for a time to meet its creditors, and secondly that in consequence of this failure he became a brewer in Hampshire. He longed to keep these two items from the world because he wanted to protect his father's name. Once he left instruction to any future biographer that he was not to mention either of these. Whether or not the book was full of error, Newman was wounded.

Perhaps Newman could never bring himself to read more than a chapter or two of Mozley's book. But other Tractarian eyes read and disliked what they found. Mozley seemed to trample on every ideal of the Movement, trivial anecdote instead of seriousness of purpose, brash judgment instead of charity. 'Culling Eardley Smith was then at Oriel, very much the same ridiculous personage as he always was, and a flagrant tuft-hunter' (1, 105). 'Theodore Williams was not only a very cantankerous but also a very ridiculous person in any religious reckoning' (1, 99). Hinds, later Bishop of Norwich, is called 'poor Hinds'—'I think there was just a suspicion of craziness' (1, 271). 'Poor Reid'— 'after a not unsuitable marriage' he 'threw himself from a window at Venice into the canal' (1, 49). Professor Hampden 'stood before you like a milestone, and brayed at you like a jackass' (1, 380); W. G. Ward, keeping his Lenten fast by lying in bed till 11 a.m. with a large dish of mutton chops warming at his fire (1, 411). Mozley was almost as bad about colleges—the degradation of St. Edmund Hall, the Fellows of Magdalene who desired no addition to their knowledge and ideas, for 'they were incapable of it' (1, 60); a former Fellow of Oriel who has an angry eye and a carbunculous complexion (1, 348).

No more quotations are needed, though more might be given to show why Mozley's book was not seen as a good history of the Oxford Movement or a good history of anything else. It was brash.

The Oxford Movement was everything that was not brash in religion; quiet, dedicated, sacramental, concentrated, never superficial, never noisy, never gossipy.

Newman is the very core. He is everything, in Mozley's book. That is not easy to see, because Newman hated the book; and because his person

is half hidden behind a cloud of gossip, and Common Room anecdotes, and malicious asides. But
he is the core. When you read the book with
clearer eye, you see why Newman's sister liked
what she read.

Newman was a genius, surrounded by yapping
curs. Men said he was insincere. No one was more
sincere. Men said he was a mere orator. Nothing
could be more untrue, he minded about what he
said and not how he said it. They still remembered the gait, the rapid movement, the stooping
head. He had a restless energy, a pale face, lus-
trous eyes. He always wore a long tail coat, and it
became the badge of his school. He was always
busy, yet always found time for the man who
needed him. He looked to encourage everything
that was promising in his younger friends, and
put his expectations of them high, sometimes too
high. He had a faith in providence so strong that
he applied it to the trivial circumstances and
changes of life. He was interested in the varieties
of human character and loved to study its diversity, and asked himself of this or that young man,
what is he good for? What will he do best? He
loved nature, trees and flowers, sky and cloud—
Mozley says a strange thing of him, 'he carried his
scenery with him' (1, 214).

So—hidden among the trivialities, and irrele-
vances, and side-swipes at worthies, some still
living—the book had a hero; Mozley's own old
hero and long-parted friend.

The surviving leaders of the Oxford Movement
found Mozley's book a degradation for the Movement. But only one of the leaders survived. Gay,
hard-riding Hurrell Froude died of consumption
forty-six years before. John Keble, dear humorous retiring pastor and poet, died sixteen years
before. Pusey remained; in his last two months of

life; with the reputation, great or controversial, of one who held the heirs of the Oxford Movement together through the terrible times of the forties and fifties.

Mozley's book began to obsess Pusey. He could think of nothing else. He returned to it again and again. He started destroying old letters, to stop this sort of thing happening again. Did it not show the dire need for a true history of the Oxford Movement—accurate, sympathetic, discriminating? A month before he died, he chose his man. Church should do it; he could write history; he understood humanity; he had lived amid the events. He was the only living historian qualified to do the job.

In 1885 (or perhaps in 1884) Church began to write. Perhaps he wrote because dying Pusey laid on him so solemn a charge. Perhaps he wrote because he too found Mozley's book trivial, and whatever else the Oxford Movement was, it was not trivial. In the unpublished papers we see a third reason. Mrs. Hawkins asked him to edit her dead husband's papers. Church disliked Hawkins and had no such intention. But he read the papers. And he did not like what he found. There he saw the Oxford Movement seen from the other side; and it seemed to be misrepresented by shallow minds. We remember the phrases of the book he wrote in the end—how they were men too small to understand the moral stature which they met.

He did not publish. Years went by. He did not even finish. He died before he finished. Why? He was not a dithering author by nature. He normally finished what he started.

Ought he to publish? He had the charge from Pusey. but he must have had qualms. He was not the only person to have qualms. On October 19, 1888, the historian Lord Acton went for a walk in

the grounds of Hawarden Castle, the home of Mr.
Gladstone. He walked with his host, and with
Liddon, Dr. Pusey's friend and biographer. They
argued, should Church publish his essays on the
Oxford Movement? Acton said that he was 'not
against' the publishing. *Not against* is not a phrase
to portray enthusiasm. Certainly Acton was luke-
warm. But Acton believed, and said then, that
Church would not publish these papers so long as
Newman was alive. (Liddon's diary *ad diem*.)

This is a true explanation. Biographers do not
publish the lives of their subjects while that subject lives. Church was not writing a biography, he
was writing a history. But for him this history
was almost a single person. Church outlived Newman by less than four months.

Tractarian spirituality had an enchanting atmo-
sphere. Part of this enchantment was *reserve*. It
disliked what was flamboyant. It shrank from religion in the market-square. It was not fond of the
seeking of publicity. It liked to hide from the gaze
of men or women who could not understand. Religion was very sacred, too sacred to be cast among
swine. They were quiet men. Stay away from too
much traffic with the world and say your prayers.
Keble, remote in his village parish in Hampshire,
was the type. Isaac Williams, gentle otherworldly
poet and curate in Gloucestershire, was another of
the type. This reserve was continuous with much
that was best in the English religious tradition:
Hooker tending sheep in his field, George Herbert
and his pastor, William Law and his retired prayer-
fulness at King Cliffe. But in the Oxford Movement
it had a new edge: against worldliness, whether
within the world or the Church. Something was
Puritan, at times something even hard, about the
shrinking from the display of the self. But it fitted
English ideas of courtesy.

Now when we consider this deep devotional reserve in the disciples of the Oxford Movement, and then contemplate Richard Church sitting down to write, we are brought up sharp. Church was a man like Keble, or Isaac Williams; dedicated to the idea of reserve, because of the sacredness of religious truth and the abnegation of the self. Yet this Oxford Movement that he set out to describe was entangled with his deepest feelings and faith.

To write about that or those to whom you owe the best of your religion is a grateful task. Because it was a grateful task Church succeeded in writing a classic. But to write about those to whom you owe deep debts is very difficult without being engaged personally, for the memories carry echoes in one's own soul. And that is what made Church's task awkward, and why in the end the book's stature may be found to be more in literature than in history. And we see that part of the reason is the devotion of a Tractarian, the reluctance to expose his soul. We do not forget that he never published it; that he went on brooding over the text and died before he was satisfied that he could publish.

The ground began to be occupied. Other men with memories printed. And one of them disturbed Church a little. It was Dean Burgon's *Lives of Twelve Good Men*, published in 1888, just posthumously. It is a delightful book, and Church could not quite like all that he read therein.

Burgon was much less of a journalist, but he also was a gossiper and anecdotalist, more charming than Mozley and closer to the truth. His book pinpointed the fundamental difficulty of all this historical endeavor, the difficulty that made Church so uneasy as he drafted. Here was a religious movement and its leader, deserted for reasons still unintelligible. The essence of the problem was the true place of Newman in what happened. For Church as for Tom Mozley, this was the only problem that counted.

Burgon had a short and easy way, throughout his life, with every doubt or difficulty that confronted him. Not in all the Victorian age was there another man who knew his mind so resolutely. To his difficulty over Newman, Burgon had a simple solution. The Oxford Movement was founded and led by a Cambridge man, Hugh James Rose; so far as it may be ascribed to any one man. It was like a great river, with its origins in many little streams and sources. But there was a single 'authoritative voice,' a single 'commanding figure,' 'conspicuous beyond the rest.' The Oxford Movement was not started by Newman, its course was influenced but not led by him, his disappearance in 1845 made small difference to its development. By what book will Newman be specially remembered? Perhaps, one might think, the *Parochial Sermons*; or the *Essay on Development*; or *The Idea of a University*; or the *Apologia*? None of these, said Burgon, but the *Arians of the Fourth Century,* an obscure, incomplete book of early life, showing more promise than performance (Burgon, *Lives,* p. 88). Burgon did not doubt Newman's sincerity or his truthfulness. But he doubted his loyalty (p. 163) and criticized his 'extravagances' (p. 136, cf. 165). He allowed him to be a charming gentleman; to possess an exquisite felicity of style (p. 411); to preach fair sermons and to be the only preacher in Oxford who could keep Charles Marriott awake in a university sermon (p. 183); but he called his conversion by the name of *desertion* (p. 161), and quoted a fierce attack by Newman's successor at St. Mary's, in the phrase *Intense unconscious love of power* (p. 409).

The appearance, and the success, of this second book of Oxford Movement anecdotes hurt Richard

Church. He disliked the book. He was much vexed by letters to the *Times* about the book (Liddon's Diary, Oct. 10, 1889). Commissioned, almost as a sacred task, to write the authentic history of the Movement he could not but feel that his book, if it ever appeared, would be only one among scores of books on the same subject. One of his draft essays was a portrait of Newman's disciple Charles Marriott. One of Burgon's twelve good men was Charles Marriott. Church must have asked himself, what was he doing spending this time?

*   *   *   *   *   *   *

To wait till your main subject is dead—

To see everyone else occupying the ground and occupying it with error—

To doubt whether what you are doing is necessary, or even right—

To wonder whether it can be the part of a wise man to expose the folly or wickedness of heads of Oxford Colleges whose widows might still live—

To be a man of reserve, and reticence, and to hold this reticence as part of your spiritual and devotional ideal, and yet to realize that if you write this book you cannot but be writing autobiography—

Still, it is odd not to finish. And there is no doubt of the basic reason. To publish was too painful. He had loved the highest ideals; he had never deserted them; but he had seen them condemned, and mocked, and made to collapse, precious affections trampled by the boots of uncomprehending minds. It was suffering to finish. He never finished. Edward Talbot begged him not to leave it there; here was a movement that changed the face of English religion and yet he left it at the moment of failure. He would not alter. He made no attempt to add. That was what it was: failure.

And this is the stature, the depth, of this classic book. Reluctantly, because Pusey asked him, because he was disturbed by the errors of others, he pushed his way, hesitantly, up the hill; and when he got to the top he could not leave, because he found it a kind of hill of crucifixion.

So I have taken a single instance of a disciple of the Oxford Movement; and shown that half a century later it still pained him to write about it, because the memories plucked at his heart. Here is a proof, if historical proof is possible in such an intangible quality, of the highest possible idealism, and its real effects, in individuals who came under its influence; an idealism that is the rational ground for celebration of this memory today.

Notes

Chapter 1: Anglicanism: A Church Adrift?

[1]Baron Friedrich von Hügel, *Selected Letters* 1896–1924 (London: J. M. Dent & Sons Ltd, 1927), p. 220.
[2]Ibid., p. 174.
[3]Ibid., p. 261.
[4]Walter Pater in a review of *Robert Elsmere* in the Guardian, quoted by Geoffrey Faber in *Jowell* (Cambridge, Mass.: Harvard University Press, 1957), p. 382.
[5]Herbert Hensley Henson, *Retrospect of an Unimportant Life*, Vol. 2 (Oxford: Oxford University Press, 1943), p. 253.

Chapter 2: The Anglican Theological Tradition

[1]*Documents of Vatican II*, tr. & ed. W. M. Abbott (Herder & Herder, 1966), p. 356.
[2]*Doctrine in the Church of England*, ed. W. Temple (London: SPCK, 1938), p. 19.
[3]Ibid., new edition of 1982, p. lx.
[4]Ibid., p. 36.
[5]S. W. Sykes, *The Integrity of Anglicanism* (Mowbrays, 1978), p. 47.
[6]*Theological Freedom and Social Responsibility*, ed. S. F. Bayne (Seabury, 1967), p. 32.
[7]In his introduction to the new edition of the 1938 report, pp. lix-lx.
[8]Ibid., p. lx.
[9]*Believing in the Church*, ed. J. V. Taylor (London: SPCK, 1981), p. 4.
[10]Ibid., p. 9.
[11]Ibid., p. 167.
[12]Sykes, op. cit., p. 74.
[13]*Christ, Faith and History*, ed. S. W. Sykes and J. P. Clayton (Cambridge: Cambridge University Press, 1972).
[14]T. Cranmer, *The True and Catholic Doctrine of the Sacrament of the Lord's Body and Blood* (Thynne, 1907), p. 95.
[15]John Jewel, *An Apology of the Church of England*, in *English Reformers*, ed. T. H. L. Parker (Philadephia: Westminster Press, 1966), p. 29.
[16]Quoted in J. R. H. Moorman, *A History of the Church in England*, A. & C. Black, Third Edition, 1973, p. 234.
[17]J. H. Newman, *Apologia pro Vita Sua* (Dent, 1907), p. 133.
[18]Quoted by G. Faber, *Oxford Apostles*, 1933, p. 434.

Chapter 3: The Anglican Liturgical Tradition

[1]Henry Gee and W. J. Hardy, *Documents Illustrative of English Church History: Compiled from Original Sources* (London: Macmillan and Co., 1910), pp. 369–372; John Strype, *Memorials of the Most Reverend Father in God, Thomas Cranmer, Sometime Lord Archbishop of Canterbury. Wherein the History of the Church and the*

Reformation of It, During the Primacy of the Said Archbishop, Are Greatly Illustrated; and Many Singular Matters Relating Thereunto, Now First Published (1694). *In Three Books.*, 2 vols. (Oxford: Clarendon Press, 1812), I, 277.

[2]Lancelot Andrewes, *Opuscula quaedam posthuma* (Oxford: John Henry Parker, 1852), p. 91.

[3]See F. E. Brightman, *The English Rite: Being a Synopsis of the Sources and Revisions of the Book of Common Prayer with an Introduction and an Appendix*, 2 vols. (London: Rivingtons, 1915); E. Cardwell, *A History of Conferences and Other Proceedings Connected with the Revision of the Book of Common Prayer; from the Year 1668 to the Year 1690*, 3d ed. (Oxford: University Press, 1849); G. J. Cuming, *A History of Anglican Liturgy*, 2d ed. (London: Macmillan Press, 1982).

[4]See E. C. Ratcliff, "The Liturgical Work of Archbishop Cranmer," *The Journal of Ecclesiastical History*, VII (October, 1956), 189–203.

[5]See M. J. Hatchett, *Thomas Cranmer and the Rites of Christian Initiation* (unpublished S.T.M. thesis, General Theological Seminary, 1967).

[6]See W. D. Maxwell, *The Liturgical Portions of the Genevan Service Book* (Edinburgh: Oliver and Boyd, 1931).

[7]See J. E. Booty, *The Book of Common Prayer 1559: The Elizabethan Prayer Book* (Charlottesville: The Folger Shakespeare Library by The University Press of Virginia, 1976).

[8]See G. Donaldson, *The Making of the Scottish Prayer Book of 1637* (Edinburgh: University Press, 1954).

[9]See R. S. Bosher, *The Making of the Restoration Settlement: The Influence of the Laudians 1649–1662*, reprinted with slight revision (Westminster: Dacre Press, 1957).

[10]G. J. Cuming, *The Durham Book: Being the First Draft of the Revision of the Book of Common Prayer in 1661 Edited with an Introduction and Notes* (London: Oxford University Press, 1961).

[11]See M. J. Hatchett, *The Making of the First American Book of Common Prayer 1776–1789* (New York: Seabury Press, 1982).

[12]See W. McGarvey, *Liturgiae Americanae: or the Book of Common Prayer As Used in the United States of America Compared with the Proposed Book of 1786 and with the Prayer Book of the Church of England, and an Historical Account and Documents* (Philadelphia: Philadelphia Church Publishing Company, 1907).

[13]See E. L. Parsons and B. H. Jones, *The American Prayer Book: Its Origins and Principles* (New York: Charles Scribner's Sons, 1937); M. H. Shepherd, Jr., *The Oxford American Prayer Book Commentary* (New York: Oxford University Press, 1950).

[14]See M. J. Hatchett, *Commentary on the American Prayer Book* (New York: Seabury Press, 1980).

Chapter 5: The Oxford Movement and Its Historian

[1]Edward Denison, *Notes of My Life*, in: *Letters and Other Writings* (Kennebunkport, Me. Milford House, 1974 reprint of 1875 edition).

[2]Richard Church, *The Oxford Movement*, 1891, p. 113.

[3]*The Letters and Papers of John Henry Newman*, ed. Charles S.

Dessain (Oxford: Oxford University Press), 3:24 and 55; 5:134–135, 324.

⁴Ibid., 4:23.
⁵Ibid., 30:10–11.
⁶Ibid., see: 30:94, 99, 114–115 and 299.

The Authors

RICHARD HOLLOWAY is Rector of Church of the Advent, Boston and former rector of Old St. Paul's, Edinburgh, Scotland. He is the author of several previously published books including *Let God Arise, Beyond Belief* and *Signs of Glory*.

JOHN MACQUARRIE is Lady Margaret Professor of Divinity, Oxford and former professor of theology at Union Theological Seminary, New York City. Fr. Macquarrie is the author of numerous books including *Principles of Christian Theology* and *Twentieth Century Religious Thought*.

MARION J. HATCHETT is Professor of Liturgics and Music at the School of Theology, University of the South, Sewanee, Tennessee. He is the author of *Commentary on the American Prayer Book* and *Sanctifying Life, Time, and Space*.

MARTIN THORNTON, formerly Warden of the Community of Epiphany, is a residentiary canon of Truro Cathedral, England. Fr. Thornton's published works include *Christian Proficiency, Pastoral Theology* and *The Rock and the River*.

OWEN CHADWICK is Regius Professor of Modern History and Master of Selwyn College, Cambridge. He is the author of numerous published works in history and ecclesiastical history.